FUTURE SOUNDS

An Insider's Guide to Making and Selling Music
in the Digital Age

THIS IS A CARLTON BOOK

Design copyright © 2001 Carlton Books Limited
Text copyright © 2001 Tom Frederikse and Adrien Cook

This edition published by Carlton Books Limited 2001
20 Mortimer Street
London
W1N 7RD

A CIP catalogue for this book is available from the British
Library.

ISBN 1 84222 208 2

Art Editor: Adam Wright
Executive Editor: Terry Burrows
Design: Andy Jones
Picture Researcher: Abi Dillon
Production: Garry Lewis

Printed in Dubai

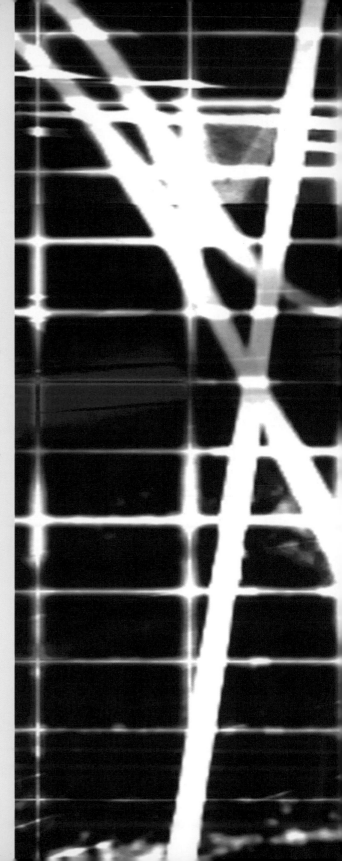

FUTURE SOUNDS

An Insider's Guide to Making and Selling Music
in the Digital Age

Tom Frederikse
and
Adrien Cook

CARLTON
BOOKS

CONTENTS

Manifesto   6
Introduction: A Guide To The 21st Century Music Business   8

Chapter 1:   Basic Stuff   14
Chapter 2:   MIDI Sequencing   22
Chapter 3:   Digital Sampling   34
Chapter 4:   Mixing Desks   52
Chapter 5:   Fairy Dust And Magical Effects   64
Chapter 6:   The Final Mix   80
Chapter 7:   Live Recording   94
Chapter 8:   The Recording Studio In Your Computer   114
Chapter 9:   Setting Up Your Own Studio   124
Chapter 10:   Selling Your Music   142

Appendix A: A Basic Recording Session   160
Appendix B: PCs for Idiots   163
Appendix C: How To Be A Mac Man   165
Appendix D: Making The Leap To Macintosh   167
Appendix E: Useful Websites   170
Appendix F: Charts: Beats Per Minute And Time Stretch   171
Appendix G: The Top 40 Frequently Asked Questions   174
Appendix H: Glossary   177

Index   188
Acknowledgements   192

MANIFESTO

"**Knowledge is Power**." *It's* true *for politicians and spies,* and these *days* it's **true for musicians** *too.* The music business *of the early* **21st** *century is just now* **beginning** *to reveal its* *nature* *and its name is* **"D.I.Y."**

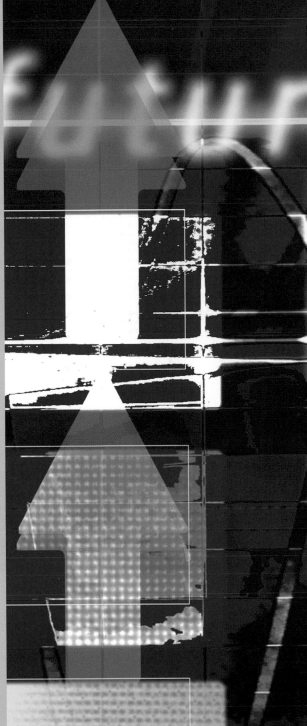

INTRODUCTION
THE SOUND OF THE 21ST CENTURY

A New Set Of Values

The 1990s killed off many of the biggest names in show business. The likes of CBS, Chrysalis, Virgin and Island no longer exist as autonomous record companies. Even three of the six so-called "major labels" have been absorbed into the other four international media conglomerates: Warner, Sony, BMG and Unigram. Smaller record companies with a long-standing tradition of functioning as talent scouts for the major labels have been forced to pioneer new media such as the Internet and MP3 to sell their music. With a heavy reduction in the volume of companies operating, the number of active talent scouts – the good old "A&R" men – has equally dwindled. Only the most widely and loudly hyped gigs have A&R types in attendance. Accordingly, the traditional ways of getting noticed are now becoming increasingly ineffective.

Fewer companies means fewer (and more insecure) staff. With A&R jobs rapidly vanishing, labels are increasingly tending towards playing it safe. In a business as risky as the commercial music world, this creates an uncomfortable tension

Musician/DJ Fat Boy Slim has helped to blur the line between pop star and DJ.

between those wanting to discover new music and bands, and those wanting to sign only the tested and proven styles. Of course, exciting new groups still manage to break through, but sterile, prefabricated pop acts now get more attention than ever before.

Of course, this doesn't mean that there's less music being sold – on the contrary, sales of CDs and cassettes are now higher than ever. Indeed, the number of records sold in any week in 2000 far exceeds the wildest dreams of any record label back in the 1960s. Furthermore, the record market has expanded to cover virtually every country on earth. Pop music has found new life in film soundtrack albums, music TV channels and computer games. Hit songs are used to sell

The music industry loves to recycle. Thirty years after they split up, the Beatles produced the top-selling album of 2000.

everything from beer to political parties. Even advertising agencies are getting in on the act by producing hit singles.

Hot Competition

The problem with this seemingly healthy picture is in the mathematics: whilst overall sales of records have rocketed, so too has the volume of music being produced. During the 1960s, in any week when a Beatles tune was at the top of the charts, between 20 and 60 singles were released. All of them were competing for places in the Top 40. In recent years, the number of records released in the UK has risen to as high as 600 in a single week. Since the number of chart vacancies has remained at 40, it's self evident that the competition for each position has severely intensified.

With so many bands and musicians vying for such limited limelight, the job of the record company has become a far less geographical one. Many label bosses now see little need to send talent scouts outside of their offices when more and more music simply finds its own way to their desks. Furthermore, this new music is being produced to a vastly higher standard than it was even a decade ago. After all, what's the incentive to send out A&R staff or hire expensive studios to re-record demos when the finished product is already there for the taking? So what does all this mean for the budding pop star? It's simple: He or she needs to get clued up.

Brian Wilson may have been a musical genius but God only knows what would have happened to the Beach Boys if he'd acted as their lawyer or accountant. Our advice: STICK TO THE MUSIC.

Over the years, many pundits have implored would-be pop stars to learn business, law or accounting. The conventional wisdom was that if music was a business then musicians must become businessmen. DON'T BELIEVE IT. In most cases musicians make lousy shopkeepers. Few musicians can fully understand, let alone negotiate, their own contracts. That's what lawyers and accountants are for. When getting clued up, stay closer to home.

The First Rule

Technology has come a long way, baby.

The record company mindset has changed and adapted to this new buyer's market. No longer does an artist have to endure the torture of the record company assigning a never-ending queue of producers to record and mix his music – often to the musician's dislike. No longer do record companies create and control the artist's sound to the point of excluding the artist himself.

In this brave new world, any aspiring artist begins (and usually finishes) the recording process alone. He operates the recording devices himself (even while playing) and mixes his own record. He makes the editorial decisions and probably "burns" his

It may sound obvious, but when trying to sell something you should always make it THE BEST YOU POSSIBLY CAN. This doesn't mean that you have to spend huge amounts of money – music of the highest technical quality can now be made in anyone's front room and can compete directly with music made in the most expensive studios.

Consider these facts: the second most costly item traditionally used to record pop music – the tape recorder – is no longer necessary; the most expensive item – the mixing desk – is increasingly less crucial and becoming obsolete in its traditional form.

Through the widespread use of computers, the ritual of recording and processing large numbers of "tracks" has become easily accessible and accessibly cheap. The once-complex process of creating and mixing music has been wrenched from the technician's grip and placed in the public domain. Of course, the creative requirement hasn't changed – you still have to have that "something" – but the technical skills are now well within the grasp of anyone with a few brain cells.

The Fairlight music computer – the first modern sampling system.

US-born Moby made independent label Mute financially strong with his "sleeper" album Play.

own CD at the end of the session. All of these tasks are relatively simple and can be achieved for a fraction of what used to be considered a small record deal. In many cases the most difficult part of the process is finding a suitable room to pump up the volume. And, of course, that perennial chestnut of coming up with a half-decent idea.

But if this is all uncharted territory how do you get off the starting blocks? Well here's the good news: *Future Sounds* will teach you what you need to know and how to avoid what you don't need to know. So let's get going!

CHAPTER 1
BASIC ST

Sound Sources

It may seem obvious, but it's important first to get a clear understanding of the different types of sound that you may want to use in your recordings. Sounds can come from a large number of sources, but all of them fall under one of five principal categories.

1. Microphones

Sounds that occur naturally in the air – those which we can hear without any artificial assistance – must be recorded with a traditional microphone. The most basic source is the human voice, which is always recorded using a microphone aimed somewhere in the vicinity of the person's mouth. The microphone transforms the sound you hear into an electronic signal which travels through the studio equipment before being converted back into audible sound by the loudspeakers. Sound recorded with a microphone has to be stored in some way so that it can be played back – either through the traditional methods of tape-recording and vinyl records, or through some sort of digital recording onto a computer disk. The signal coming out of a microphone is invariably extremely weak and therefore is susceptible to interference when long cables or wireless connections are used, so don't use unnecessarily long cables.

2. Guitars and Basses

Instruments with magnetic pick-ups include electric guitars, bass guitars, or suitably fitted acoustic instruments such as classical guitars and violins. Such instruments always have a "jack" plug socket fitted somewhere to the body which allows them to be connected directly to the mixing desk (usually via a DIRECT INJECTION BOX). Once

UFF

The bass guitar is only one of a number of possible sound sources that you might well wish to use with your recordings. It is usually plugged directly into a mixing desk.

again, the signal from these sockets is usually quite weak and similarly susceptible to interference if long leads are used.

3. Synthesizers and Electronic Keyboards

This category covers a wide range of musical instruments including electronic organs and electric pianos. Traditional synthesizers are electronic machines that make noises via tone generators that can be cleverly filtered to sound like other instruments. Synthesizers have all of their sounds readily available inside. They can be connected to the mixing desk via JACK sockets (or in some cases XLR microphone-type sockets). The signal is generally

This selection of jack, phono and XLR plugs covers the connection needs of most commonly used audio equipment.

very strong, so it's a good idea to turn the volume down before you play a note.

4. Digital Samplers

Samplers are often thought of as synthesizers, but there is one very fundamental difference: while synthesizers generate their own sounds, most fresh-out-of-the-box samplers make no noise whatsoever until you put sounds into them. A sampler allows you to create and manipulate your own sounds which can be loaded into the machine either by using a microphone, sounds generated from another electronic source (electric guitar, keyboard, CD player, turntable), or by using pre-recorded sounds. Samplers can be connected to a mixing desk or recording machine in the same way as synthesizers.

5. Feedback

This is not strictly a sound source, but it certainly will act like one at the most inopportune moments in your recording career. Everyone knows the terrible obnoxious whine of feedback that comes when a microphone is held too close to a connected loudspeaker. Digital feedback and in-line feedback will occur when an electronic or digital signal is directly connected in a loop to its own source, leaving the signal to go round and round.

Beware: all feedback signals are extremely powerful, and they usually get stronger by the second. The message here is simple: IF YOU VALUE YOUR SPEAKERS (AND YOUR EAR DRUMS) PULL DOWN THE VOLUME FADER AS SOON AS POSSIBLE – IF NOT QUICKER.

An industry standard – the Akai S3000 stereo MIDI sampler.

Studio Overview

Solid State Logic produce some of the greatest desks of them all.

A recording studio can be a daunting sight to the uninitiated, so let's make things easy by breaking it down into its core elements.

The Mixing Desk

Traditionally, the heart of the studio is the mixing desk. This is where the different sound sources are connected, combined, sonically refined and balanced. The mixing desk can be likened to an electronic orchestral conductor – it is the overall controller with the power to strengthen or silence any chosen instrument. Whether the mixing desk is a state-of-the-art 96-channel, sloped and lighted console or a tiny 4-channel box, it remains the nerve centre of any studio.

But things are beginning to change in this area. The mammoth wooden and metal mixing desk of old has started to give way to the "virtual mixing desk" located on a hard disk. As you might expect, the computer-based version can do everything the old one could do, and much more besides. Some computer mixing desks exist entirely on the screen with just a mouse to manipulate the controls. More sophisticated models – such as the ProTools ProControl – have real, hands-on faders with which you can manually control the virtual desk.

One of the most innovative studios ever built — Real World Studios in Bath, England.

Affordable, efficient and noise-free, the highly rated Mackie company have produced some of the most popular mixing desks of the past decade.

Recording Devices

All sound sources being used on a given session must be plugged into a mixing desk, the outputs from which are then connected to some kind of recording device.

Recording equipment comes in a variety of formats. It may be a traditional tape recorder using large-spooled, magnetic tapes, perhaps allowing up to 24 separate channels of sound to be recorded either one-at-a-time or simultaneously. It may be a digital tape recorder, allowing up to 48 and even 64 separate tracks to be likewise employed. The device may be a simpler machine such as an 8-track digital recorder, using small cassette-type cartridges. Increasingly, however, the most likely recording

Big console = big money.

device to be used is a computer. Digital recordings can be made directly onto a computer's hard disk and stored permanently on CD-ROMs. This so-called "direct-to-disk" digital recording allows for unlimited and quick editing of sounds and performances, thereby making the creation of your own music accessible and affordable.

Monitoring the Sound

For you to be able to hear what you are doing, the mixing desk must be connected to some sort of amplification and loudspeaker system. This part of the equation is all too often relegated to an afterthought. Don't make this basic mistake. Use a good quality amplifier – it doesn't have to be an expensive model – and if you must use a home stereo amp, make sure that you set the treble/bass/tone/"loudness" controls to a neutral position so that they don't affect the sound. Ideally, you should use an amp without any in-built controls – not even a volume knob (you should control this only from the mixing desk). Choose a pair of speakers that are of average quality. Super-extra-newfangled-trendy speakers might make everything sound extraordinarily good in your studio, but you may find that your music sounds dull and lifeless when played on other systems.

Sequencers

Most modern recordings – especially dance records – are created using a sequencer to generate or record the machine-based sounds, such as drum machines,

The Otari RADAR is a dedicated hard-disk recording system that is noted for its reliability.

A typical modern home recording studio.

samples and synthesizers. A sequencer can be a dedicated piece of electronic equipment or – more commonly these days – a program running on a computer. Sequencers do not generate any noise of their own, but are connected to and control external sound sources such as samplers and synthesizers.

Effects

Almost every record ever made will have used some sort of electronic effects, such as reverb, echo, delay, chorusing, flanging or equalization. Traditionally, these effects come in dedicated boxes of sophisticated electronics.

The number of effects boxes found in a studio used to be an excellent indicator of the relative wealth of the studio owner. Over the past decade, however, prices have fallen dramatically. Furthermore, more and more effects are available in "virtual" form for use with computer-based systems. Known as "plug-ins", these effects are now plentiful and common in every home studio. You can find more about effects in Chapter Five (see pages 64-79).

CHAPTER 2
MIDI SEQUEN

what is Sequencing?

Sequencing is essentially the recording of information generated from a synthesizer which can subsequently be edited and played back. No sound is actually recorded onto the sequencer, it is simply a series of instructions that tell a connected synthesizer which notes to play, when to play them, and for how long to sustain them. A good analogy is that of a music score. This tells the performer the pitch of the notes to play, the duration of each note, and the tempo at which each note should be played. It's up to the composer, performer or producer to decide on which instrument to play the notes.

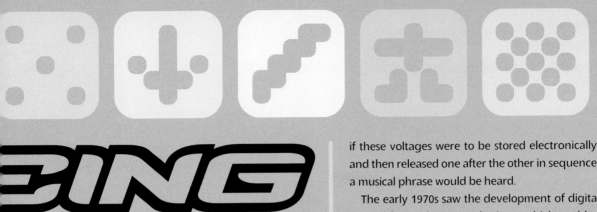

BING

Sequencers have been around since the earliest commercial synthesizers were built in the 1960s. The traditional synthesizer uses control voltages to create its sound. A series of tone generators (sometimes called "voltage-controlled oscillators" or "VCOs") electronically produce different voltages that, when amplified and sent to a loudspeaker, generate a note which is "analogous" to that variation in voltage. For example, a voltage that varies 440 times each second will produce the musical pitch "A above Middle C" on a piano keyboard. This process is known as "analogue synthesis".

In practice, the pitch of a VCO can be controlled from a keyboard which has been designed to produce a different voltage according to which key has been depressed. Similarly, the duration of the voltage and resulting sound depends on how long the key has been held. It doesn't take a huge leap of imagination to see that if these voltages were to be stored electronically, and then released one after the other in sequence, a musical phrase would be heard.

The early 1970s saw the development of digital control for analogue synthesizers, which enabled computers to be used to process information with great precision. This led directly to the birth of the digital sequencer and, later, the first generation of fully digital instruments. But because the different manufacturers used their own methods for controlling their instruments, compatibility was a problem. It was clear that some sort of universal standard was needed to enable different products to "talk" to one other. And so it was that in the early 1980s the Musical Instrument Digital Interface (MIDI) was born. This enabled several instruments produced by different manufacturers to be played from a single keyboard.

Kraftwerk were pioneers in the use of pre-MIDI sequencing.

About Midi

MIDI was instantly popular with keyboard players and programmers and developed at a rapid pace. The first mass-market MIDI sequencer was the four-track Yamaha QX1. When combined with a KX88 "mother" keyboard and the TX816 MIDI sound module, self-contained four-channel recordings became possible without any sound ever needing to recorded on tape. Other manufacturers quickly followed suit and pretty soon the five-pin MIDI "IN", "OUT" and "THRU" sockets were commonplace on all electronic musical instruments.

During the same period, personal computers had also been developing in leaps and bounds. It wasn't long before MIDI sequencing software started to appear. Many new software companies quickly emerged, such as Steinberg (Pro 12 software) Gerhard Lengehling (Lengehling Supertrack for the Commodore 64), UMI (for the BBC Model B), and Opcode and Mark of The Unicorn, writing programs for the revolutionary new Apple Macintosh. By the time the Atari ST with built-in MIDI ports appeared in 1987, MIDI was a fact of life for most musicians.

It doesn't take a particularly powerful computer to run a MIDI sequencer. Although the early systems were somewhat unstable and prone to crashing, the Atari ST with its meagre one megabyte of Random Access Memory (RAM) became the workhorse for thousands of musicians, engineers and producers. In fact, many are still in use today and are held in high esteem for their simplicity, accurate MIDI timing, and tight "grooves".

MIDI In Practice

MIDI is fundamentally very simple to use. Most devices are fitted with three MIDI sockets – IN, OUT and THRU. Each of these MIDI ports is capable of carrying 16 channels of MIDI information. You simply connect the MIDI OUT from your computer's MIDI interface to the MIDI IN of your keyboard, and the MIDI OUT from your keyboard to the MIDI IN of your computer MIDI interface. The MIDI THRU socket simply passes on any information arriving at the MIDI IN socket, so that it can be routed to the MIDI IN socket on a second keyboard or sound module. This process is known as DAISYCHAINING. A variety of commonly used MIDI set-ups is show in the diagrams across the page.

Most modern MIDI-equipped synthesizers and sound modules are MULTITIMBRAL. This means that they can generate more than one sound at a time. Indeed, many can now process 16 parts simultaneously by assigning a MIDI channel to each different sound.

Multiple Ports

If you have more than two or three MIDI sound modules it is a good idea to invest in a multi-port MIDI interface. Such units allow your software to access a number of different MIDI inputs and outputs, each one being capable of carrying 16 independent MIDI channels. This allows you to assign each of MIDI module to its own port. There are several benefits to this approach:

- You don't have to disable MIDI channels on one module to stop it playing sequencer parts intended for another module.
- Your MIDI modules will be arranged in a "star network", meaning that their individual response times will be much faster than a daisychained network. This will make your music much tighter.
- Most multi-port interfaces have SMPTE inputs and outputs. SMPTE is a "timecode" that enables you to synchronize your MIDI sequencer with external tape recorders or video machines.

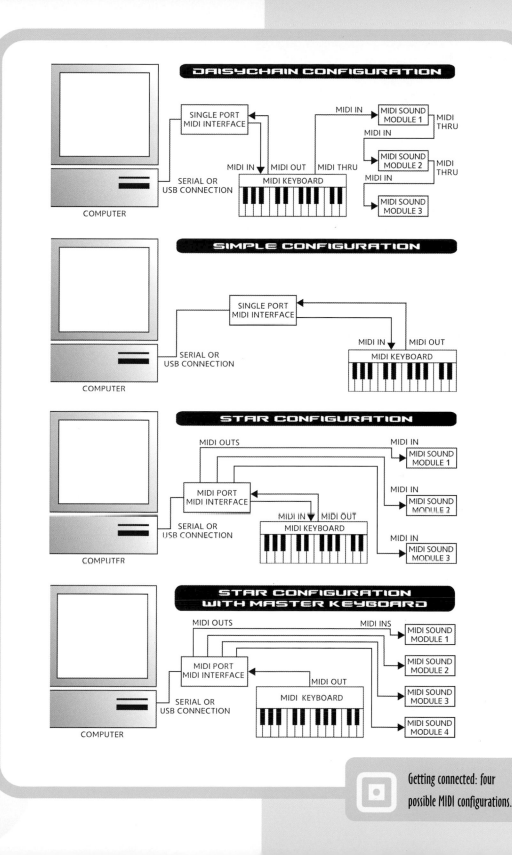

Getting connected: four possible MIDI configurations.

Using The Software

Let's now take a look at a typical MIDI software sequencer in practice. Although there are many different programs from which you can choose, they all work in broadly the same way.

Cubase VST (Virtual Studio Technology) is the latest incarnation of a sequencing program first developed by the German company Steinberg in 1989. Over the next few pages you'll see an outline of some of the program's key features. If you are already a Cubase user don't worry if the images don't look identical to those on your computer screen: even though Cubase comes in a variety of forms, the basics remain the same.

The Arrange Window

At the heart of Cubase VST is the much-copied, cut-and-paste Arrange Window. When this first appeared it was revolutionary in that it enabled

Cubase VST Arrange Window.

musicians to see the whole arrangement of their song in a graphical format, with the tracks running down the vertical axis and elapsed time (either measured in "real" time or musical bars) along the horizontal axis. Each MIDI individual track appears on the window as a horizontal bar, indicating the points at which the performance begins and ends. Segments from any (or all) of these tracks can be cut, copied or dragged, and pasted to any other location in the song's Arrange Window. Furthermore, performances could be modified afterwards using the features of the Cubase Toolbox (*see page 31*).

Essential Cubase

Recording a song in Cubase is simplicity itself. The beauty of the Arrange Window is that it allows you to see the overall structure of the song, while still giving you access to any part (or even any single note) at any point in time. This window will automatically appear each time you run the Cubase VST program.

You will also notice a second smaller window on the screen. This is the Transport Window which makes the sequencer "run". Rather like the controls of a tape recorder, you can record, play back, fast forward and rewind at different points in the song. These two windows contain everything you need to record your first MIDI track. (Note: on some versions of Cubase the Transport Window may appear as a part of the Arrange Window.)

1. From the Arrange Window, select any of the default tracks in the INSTRUMENT column. This is the track on which you will be able to record.

2. Click and hold on the TRACK NAME to reveal the choice of MIDI channels (each one can represent a different sound) and select one. You should now be able to hear your chosen sound when you play the keyboard.

Steps 3 to 9 refer to control parameters found in the Transport Window.

3. To choose a tempo (the speed of the music you want to play), double-click on TEMPO and enter a number in beats-per-second. Hit the return key. (Most modern electronic dance music averages out at around 120-160 beats per minute).

4. Set the LEFT and RIGHT LOCATORS by double-clicking on each one individually and entering the number of the bar. The locators set the start and end positions of your recording. Typically you could choose 1 and 3 to create a two-bar recording, 1 and 5 (for four bars), or 1 and 9 (for an eight-bar cycle).

5. Click on the CYCLE icon so that it is highlighted. This will loop the sequence between the two bars selected within the LEFT and RIGHT LOCATORS.

6. Click on the CLICK icon so that it is highlighted. This gives you a metronome sound to help you play in time. The speed of the click can be varied by altering the TEMPO as shown in step 3.

7. Click on the RECORD button, wait for the four-beat count-in, and then start jamming.

8. When you hit the STOP button, a long, rectangular bar will appear on the screen. This box represents the performance you've just recorded.

9. To play back the music you have just recorded, click on the PLAY button. Each time the vertical cursor line scrolls over the rectangular bar, it will play back the notes you recorded on the selected MIDI channel.

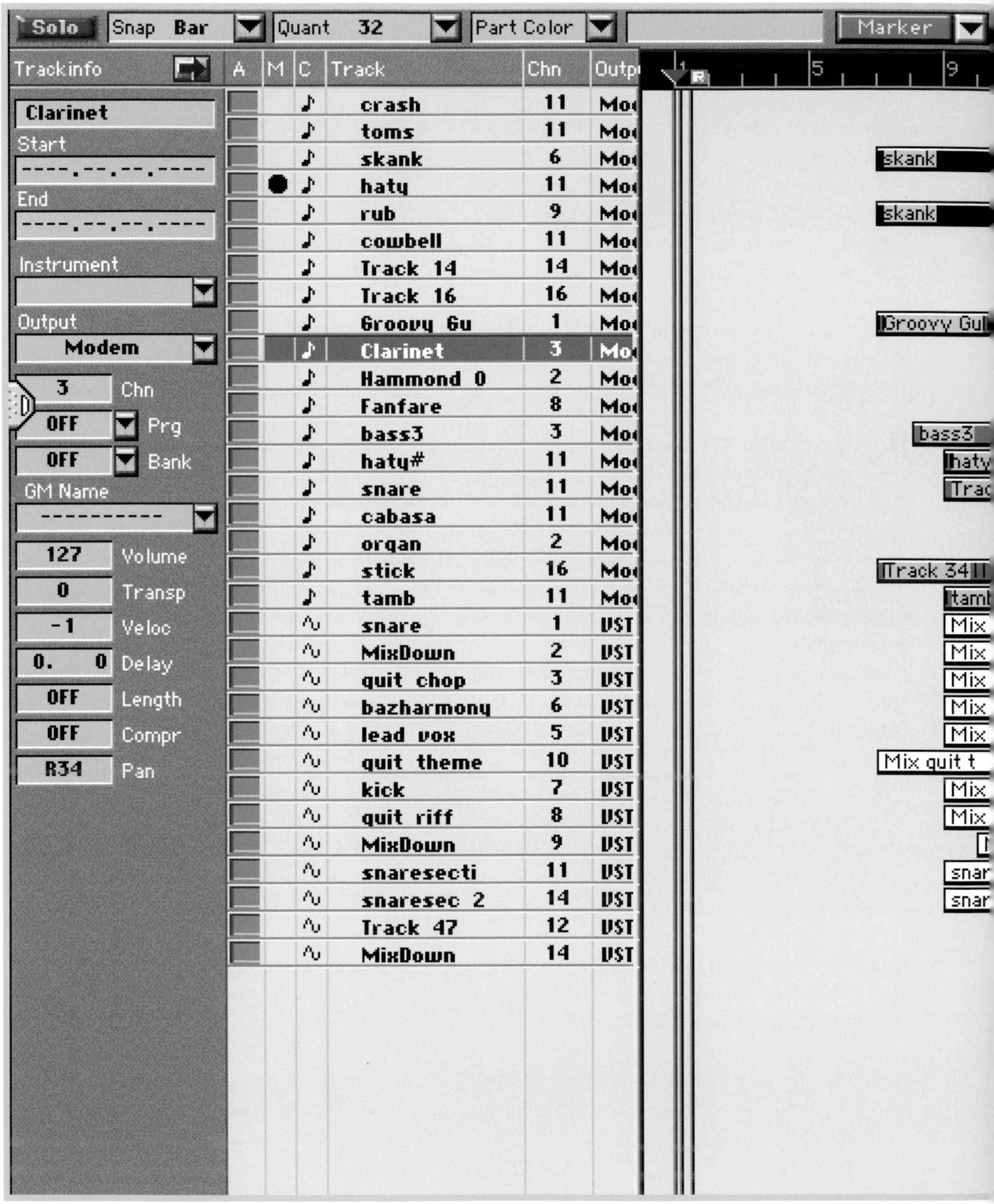

| Solo | Snap | Bar | ▼ | Quant | 32 | ▼ | Part Color | ▼ | | | Marker | ▼ |

Trackinfo ➡

A	M	C	Track	Chn	Outp		1 R		5		9
		♪	crash	11	Mod						
		♪	toms	11	Mod						
		♪	skank	6	Mod			skank			
	●	♪	haty	11	Mod						
		♪	rub	9	Mod			skank			
		♪	cowbell	11	Mod						
		♪	Track 14	14	Mod						
		♪	Track 16	16	Mod						
		♪	Groovy Gu	1	Mod			Groovy Gu			
		♪	Clarinet	3	Mod						
		♪	Hammond 0	2	Mod						
		♪	Fanfare	8	Mod						
		♪	bass3	3	Mod			bass3			
		♪	haty#	11	Mod			haty			
		♪	snare	11	Mod			Trac			
		♪	cabasa	11	Mod						
		♪	organ	2	Mod						
		♪	stick	16	Mod			Track 34			
		♪	tamb	11	Mod			tamb			
		∿	snare	1	VST			Mix			
		∿	MixDown	2	VST			Mix			
		∿	quit chop	3	VST			Mix			
		∿	bazharmony	6	VST			Mix			
		∿	lead vox	5	VST			Mix			
		∿	quit theme	10	VST			Mix quit t			
		∿	kick	7	VST			Mix			
		∿	quit riff	8	VST			Mix			
		∿	MixDown	9	VST						
		∿	snaresecti	11	VST			snar			
		∿	snaresec 2	14	VST			snar			
		∿	Track 47	12	VST						
		∿	MixDown	14	VST						

Trackinfo panel:

Clarinet

Start
----.--.--.----

End
----.--.--.----

Instrument
▼

Output
Modem ▼

3	Chn
OFF ▼	Prg
OFF ▼	Bank

GM Name
---------- ▼

127	Volume
0	Transp
-1	Veloc
0. 0	Delay
OFF	Length
OFF	Compr
R34	Pan

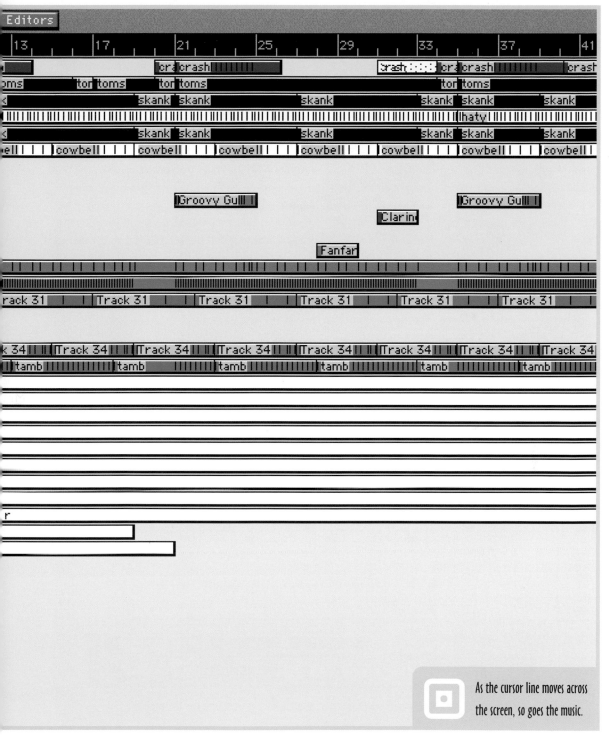

As the cursor line moves across the screen, so goes the music.

Editing Your Performance

Delving deeper into Cubase VST, the Key Edit Window (*see below*) enables you to see graphically the notes you have recorded. Each line represents a different note, the pitch of which ties to the piano keyboard on the left-hand side of the window. The start point and duration of each note is represented by the position and length of the line on the grid. As with tracks on the Arrange Window, individual notes can be moved, cut, copied and pasted to other positions.

Tightening Time

Quantization can be a life-saver if your timing skills are not up to scratch. This function allows you to "correct" a performance by automatically repositioning the notes by a preset value.

To quantize a sequence, highlight the line in the Arrange Window and click on the FUNCTIONS menu and select QUANTIZE (in some versions this may be labelled "OVER-QUANTIZE"). This command will correct your performance to the nearest 16th

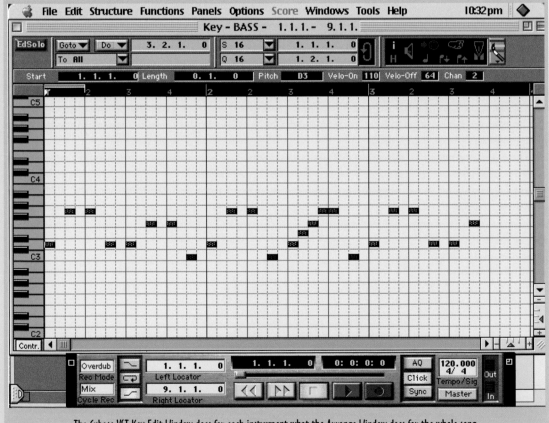

The Cubase VST Key Edit Window does for each instrument what the Arrange Window does for the whole song.

division of a bar. This value is chosen because the program's default setting is "16". To change this setting, click on the arrow in the QUANT box near the top of the window and select a new value from the drop-down menu.

Snapping

Any of the individual tracks can be moved by clicking and holding on the chosen line (in the Arrange Window) and dragging and dropping at a new location. You will notice that these boxes always fall on evenly spaced bars. This is because the SNAP function has been set to "BAR". To change this setting, click on the arrow in the SNAP box and select a new value from the drop-down menu – for example, a value of "1/2" will allow you to position the line on any half-bar interval.

The Tool Box

For easy editing, the TOOLBOX (*see left*) provides swift access to many of the functions that work with VST's various windows. These can be activated by clicking on the different icons. For example, the Scissors Tool is used for cutting parts in the Arrange Window, and the Pencil Tool is used for drawing notes in the Key Edit Window. Although the other tools are very useful they can be ignored for the time being – these are for the more seasoned Cubase traveller.

List Edit

As with most other MIDI software sequencers, the List Edit Window (*see below*) displays a detailed text list of every MIDI event recorded by the sequencer. This can is extremely useful for performing very precise edits.

Start Position		Length	Val1	Val2
1. 1. 1.	0	0. 623	C3	110
1. 1. 2.	0	0. 623	C3	110
1. 1. 3.	0	0. 623	C3	110
1. 1. 4.	0	0. 623	C3	110

The Cubase VST List Edit Window provides a numerical menu of every MIDI event recorded.

winding UP

Cubase VST is arguably the simplest program for creating quick and intuitive MIDI music. There is, of course, a great deal more to the program than the features we've just seen. But although we've only scratched the surface, you would be surprised at the number of successful musicians who use little more than these functions alone.

Other Choices

There are many other software sequencers from which you can choose. Cubase VST's main rival is E-Magic's LOGIC. This shares many features with VST, such as the Arrange, Key Edit and List Edit windows. Both of these programs come in a number of different versions, offering alternative functions and facilities depending on the price you want to pay. You can save yourself money by identifying only what you need and choosing appropriately. If, for instance, you know that you'll never need to edit and print off a music score, make sure that you are not paying extra for these functions.

Although the precise details will vary, the basic operation is the same for all computer-based MIDI sequencers. Each manufacturer has its own names and labels for the different functions, but the anatomy remains fairly constant. Think of it as if you were driving a car – each time you sit down behind a new program you may need to spend a little time finding all the controls, but soon enough you'll be up and running.

Logic's Arrange Window graphically shows where the digitally recorded music is at any point in the song. Like other MIDI recorders, the moving cursor line indicates the position on the screen as the music is played back.

Edit Functions Audio View

▽Audio 2#01

Loop
Fade In
    Curve
Fade [Out]
    Curve
Delay

▽SNARE
(Audio Object)
Icon   ☒ 〰
Dev   K12
Cha   Track 2
MIDI Cha   2
Val as   Num
Show EQs   ☒
Show Inserts ☒
Show Sends ☒
Show I/O   ☒

1 M R 〰 KIK
2 M R 〰 SNARE
3 M R 〰 HAT
4 M R 〰 RACK 1
5 M R 〰 RACK 2
6 M R 〰 FLOOR
7 M R 〰 O/H L
8 M R 〰 O/H R
9 M R 〰 BASS
10 M R 〰 LOW TOM
11 M R 〰 LOW TOM 2
12 M R 〰 TENOR SAX
13 M R 〰 Audio13
14 M R 〰 CONGA L
15 M R 〰 CONGA R
16 M R 〰 Audio16
17 M R 〰 Audio17
18 M R 〰 GTR 1
19 M R 〰 GTR 2
20 M R 〰 HAMMOND L
21 M R 〰 HAMMOND R
22 M R 〰 WURLI

01:02:49:04.66   M   120.0
80 3   2.132   373

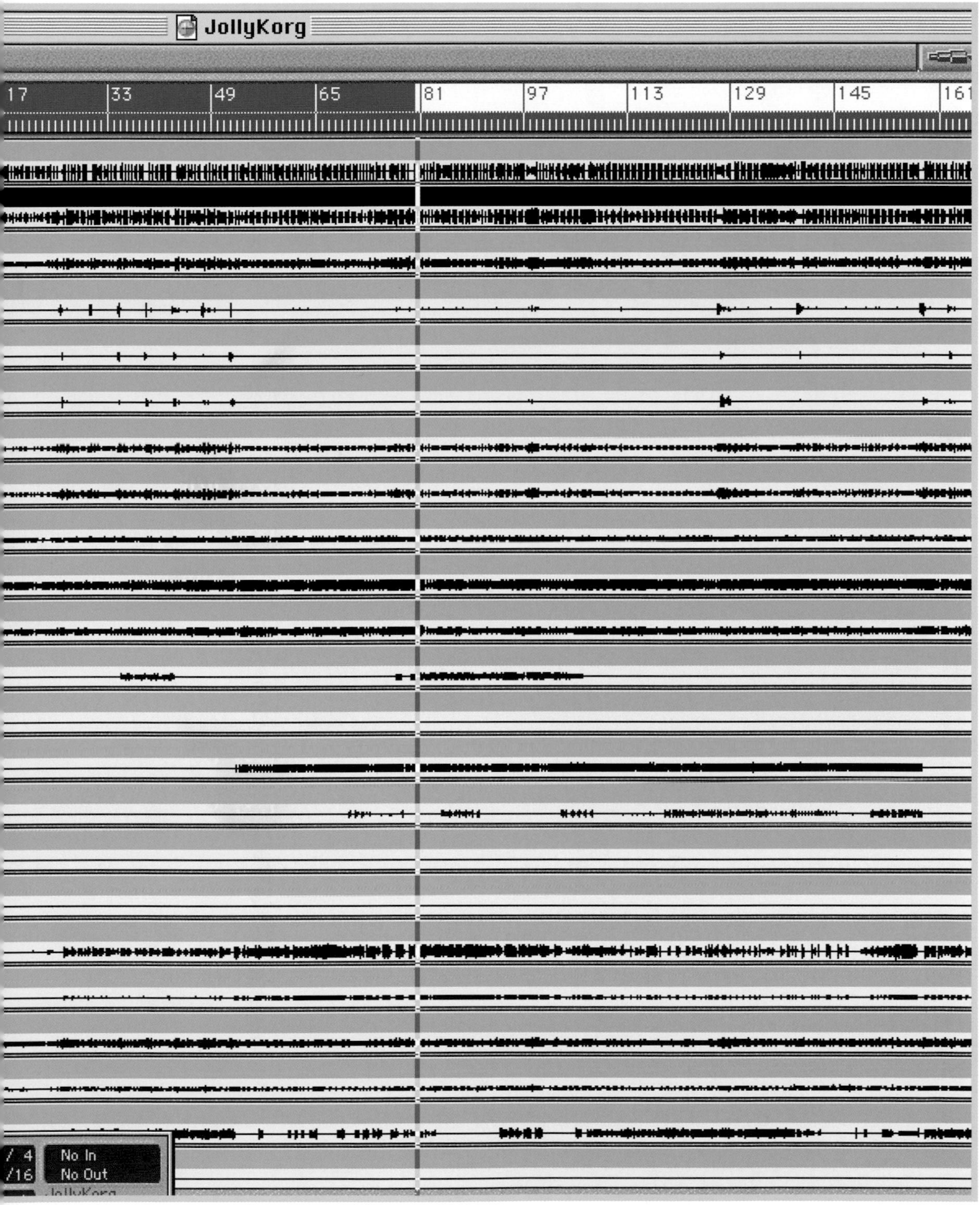
JollyKorg
17
33
49
65
81
97
113
129
145
161
No In
No Out

CHAPTER 3
DIGITAL SAMPLIN

What is Sampling?

In the world of modern music, the term SAMPLING refers to the digital recording or encoding of a sound. It can also have a number of other meanings, which can cause a bit of confusion when you're just starting out. We've all come across jargon such as the SAMPLING RATE in conjunction with CD players, which are often quoted as having "4, 8 or 16 times oversampling". What does this all mean? Stay tuned – all will be revealed.

A digital sampler is a device capable of recording sound into its on-board memory. Here it can be processed in a variety of different ways and played back from a MIDI keyboard or sequencer. We can

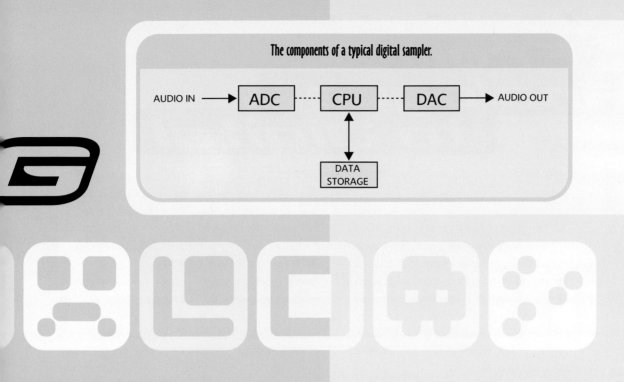

The components of a typical digital sampler.

AUDIO IN → ADC ---- CPU ---- DAC → AUDIO OUT

DATA STORAGE

break down the architecture of a sampler into four principal components:

1. Digital Conversion

The first function in a sampler's operation is to turn an audio signal into digital code. This is performed by a processor called the ANALOGUE-TO-DIGITAL CONVERTER (ADC). The ADC takes a series of high-speed snapshots of the soundwave being input and turns them into binary numbers that the sampler can understand. The number of snapshots taken each second indicates what is known as the SAMPLE RATE. In the case of a CD, this takes place 44,100 times per second (shown as is 44.1 kHz).

2. The Sampler's Brain

The CENTRAL PROCESSING UNIT (CPU) is the heart of the sampler. It contains the instrument's memory and performs the "number-crunching" necessary to manipulate the digital representation of the sound created by the ADC.

3. Playback

This modified stream of numbers is transformed into an audio signal by a DIGITAL-TO-ANALOGUE CONVERTER (DAC), which creates an analogue electrical signal that can be heard when fed into an amplifier and loudspeaker system.

4. Storing Samples

Like a regular personal computer, the sampler's processing memory is temporary. This means that it will be lost when the power is switched off. If you want to save your samples then some sort of DATA STORAGE DEVICE is also required. This is invariably provided by an hard disk drive or magneto-optical storage device which can either be in-built or connected externally.

From Analogue to Digital

During the 1960s, the technique of direct computer synthesis was first introduced. This was made possible through the development of the digital-to-analogue converter (DAC) and the availability of powerful digital computers. The DAC takes a string of numbers from the computer and turns them into a signal that can be amplified and heard through a loudspeaker. In this way, it becomes possible to input a formula for a soundwave such as a sine wave (a simple waveform of a pure tone) into the computer and hear a listenable sine wave emerge the other end. Many elaborate formulae have been developed to produce complex tones that are even capable of mimicking acoustic instruments.

Now let's reverse this process, sending a signal from a microphone through an analogue-to-digital converter – in effect a "reverse DAC". The numbers converted and stored in the computer memory are not the result of a mathematical formula, but are directly related to the sound picked up by the microphone. When that sound is played back, the DAC produces an event that should, in theory, sound like the original.

Binary Matters

Sound is a continuous medium. A pure waveform such as sine wave that has a frequency of 1 kHz means that it moves through its cycle 1000 times every second. This occurs continuously with no breaks or steps. Digital computers, on the other hand, do NOT operate in a continuous manner but instead deal with discreet steps of "0" and "1". This is the BINARY language understood by computers and other digital equipment.

Let's now give our 1 kHz sine wave a voltage swing of +1 to -1 volts. This produces a continuous wave that travels upwards by 1 volt and then downwards by the same amount, making it a smooth, simple and symmetrical shape (*see diagram across the page*). In the analogue tape medium, it's relatively easy to record and reproduce such a tone. The tape machine is switched into "record" mode, the tape rolls, and the record head magnetizes the tape. When the tape is replayed, the playback head responds to the magnetic flux pattern stored on the tape and recreates our nice, continuous sine wave.

Things are less clear-cut in the digital domain. As computers work in discreet steps, the first variable that needs to be sorted is one of RESOLUTION. This is a question of the number of separate whole pieces we should divide the sine wave voltage swing in order to reproduce it accurately: if there are too few we'll get a jagged waveform; if there are too many (which would clearly always be desirable if sound quality were the only issue), the cost of the DAC, ADC, computer memory and loss of processing speed becomes prohibitive.

The resolution can be thought of as the "width" of information that can be processed by the

A higher bit resolution means a more accurate sound reproduction.			
One-bit resolution gives	2	=	2 discreet steps
Two-bit	2^2	=	4
Three-bit	2^3	=	8
Eight-bit	2^8	=	256
Twelve-bit	2^{12}	=	4,096
Sixteen-bit	2^{16}	=	65,536

sampler. Because computers work with binary numbers this is measured in BINARY DIGITS, which are usually referred to as BITS. Looking at the chart above we can see why there is a huge difference in sound quality between an 8-bit sampler and a 16-bit sampler. The latter has 256 times greater resolution than the former. This is also significant in that the greater the resolution, the greater the DYNAMIC RANGE of the system (the difference between the quietest and loudest sounds captured). This in turn affects other important aspects such as the signal-to-noise ratio, fidelity and general "punch".

As a simple rule, the dynamic range of a sampler can be calculated by using this formula: DYNAMIC RANGE = RESOLUTION MULTIPLIED BY SIX. Thus, an 8-bit sampler will have a dynamic

range of 48 decibels (dB), while a 16-bit system has a dynamic range of 96 dB.

Our question we need to discuss is the number of snapshots or samples we need to take each second. This is the SAMPLING RATE. To get an idea of what this actually means, you can think of it as being like the number of frames-per-second being projected onto a movie screen. The more images you see each second, the higher quality the picture will be. Similarly, with digital recording, the higher the sampling rate the better the audio fidelity will be. Film and video operates at 24, 25 or 30 frames per second, which is good enough to fool the eye into thinking it is perceiving continuous movement. If that doesn't seem much, don't forget that am ordinary light bulb flashes on and off 50 times very second to create the illusion of permanent light. Unfortunately, the ear is far more critical and subjective. Consequently, a CD system has to use 44,100 snapshots per second to produce a reasonably quality sound.

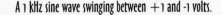

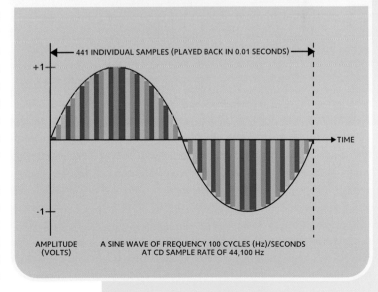

A 1 kHz sine wave swinging between +1 and -1 volts.

441 INDIVIDUAL SAMPLES (PLAYED BACK IN 0.01 SECONDS)

+1

TIME

-1

AMPLITUDE (VOLTS)

A SINE WAVE OF FREQUENCY 100 CYCLES (Hz)/SECONDS AT CD SAMPLE RATE OF 44,100 Hz

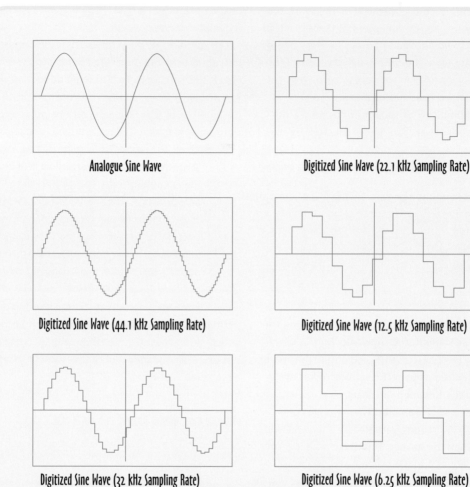

Analogue Sine Wave	Digitized Sine Wave (22.1 kHz Sampling Rate)
Digitized Sine Wave (44.1 kHz Sampling Rate)	Digitized Sine Wave (12.5 kHz Sampling Rate)
Digitized Sine Wave (32 kHz Sampling Rate)	Digitized Sine Wave (6.25 kHz Sampling Rate)

Comparison of digitized sine wave at different resolutions.

As with resolution, the sampling rate can tell us a lot about sound quality. The diagrams above show five digitized versions of the same analogue sine wave. You can see how drastically the waveform changes, especially at the lower sampling rates – 12.5 kHz and 6.25 kHz rates are extremely "lo-fi".

In practice, a waveform can be most accurately represented by using a sampling rate that is at least double the highest frequency contained within. If there are too few snapshots the recorded version will not resemble the original; too many and the memory requirements become excessive. But although accusations of quality compromise can be levelled at this aspect of digital recording, there are few people who would notice any real difference between analogue and digital sound. Nonetheless, the issue remains one of popular debate. One thing we can guarantee, though, is that sampling rates and resolutions will continue to rise as processing power becomes greater and more affordable.

Getting your Sounds

Unlike a synthesizer, a digital sampler contains no sounds of its own. It is a blank page that depends solely on your own input. This page may be filled in any way you see fit. Here are some options you might want to consider:

1. Sample CDs

Specially recorded off-the-shelf CDs can be an excellent way of getting ideas for grooves. They may also be an invaluable source of ready-to-use instruments and sounds. Sample CDs may vary in nature from simple audio files to CD-ROMs that contain data in a format recognizable to specific types of sampler. Since all of the sampling and keyboard mapping has already been done this can you save a great deal of valuable time – all you have to do is load them up. The cost of sample CDs can vary enormously from a few pounds for an audio CD to thousands for a large CD-ROM orchestral library. A word of warning: expense is no guarantee of quality, so chose cautiously.

2. Sampling from Records, CDs or Videos

This can be a highly fertile area for the samplist. Be warned, though: if you intend to use such samples in a track for commercial release on a major label, you may be wise to clear the sample with the copyright owner first. The music business is littered with the broken careers of those who didn't (and gilded with the glittering careers of those who did). You can read more about this fascinating and controversial topic on page 49.

3. Live Sampling

Although a small library of floppy disks or CD-ROMs is usually supplied with newly purchased samplers, recording your own sounds to sample remains the most creatively satisfying pursuit for most users. Sounds are frequently recorded on a small, high-quality portable recorder (most commonly DAT or MiniDisk) and subsequently sampled when back in the studio. You can have great fun banging oil drums in huge empty warehouses or disused swimming pools, recording wildebeest on the Serengeti, or anything else that you might find interesting, original or useful.

4. Sampling From Within a Song

You can generate great hooks and other interesting effects by extracting small segments from a song on which you are already working. These can be sampled, processed and then played back or sequenced within the same song. This is a foolproof way of working because you know that everything you do will fit in with the tempo and pitch of that song.

5. Creative Sound Design

It's easy to forget that although there are thousands of sample discs available (and many users never do anything more challenging than playing back CD-ROMs), using a sampler for creative sound design is usually a far more satisfying experience. Using the processing functions of any sampler you can warp your sounds into the fifth dimension.

How to Sample and Edit

As you begin a sampling session, spare a moment to think of a naming scheme for your various samples. Each and every sample must have a different name – even if they differ by just one character ("snare1" and "snare2", for instance). If you try to record a sample with the same name as an existing sample, the new recording will simply replace it and the old one will be lost forever.

CRUCIAL TIP: <u>ALWAYS</u> REMEMBER TO SAVE YOUR WORK. To avoid severe frustration, get into the habit of saving every few minutes, or at least after creating or editing each new sample.

Over the next few pages you'll find out how to use some of the features commonly found on all modern digital samplers. Let's begin by recording the sample itself.

1. Optimizing Levels

As with all audio processing, it's important to get as good a SIGNAL-TO-NOISE ratio as possible. This means getting the maximum signal with the minimum amount of noise.

Set the record level on your sampler so that it gives the maximum signal input for the sound you want to sample without CLIPPING (distorting the sound). After you have recorded the sample, if the level is too high or too low, simply do it again. If the source is too variable in volume, you can always use an external compressor to control it (*see page 68*).

Most samplers allow you to choose your own method for triggering a sample recording:

- Manually "arming" the process by pushing a button on the sampler's front panel.
- Trigger level, so that the record instruction is activated as soon as it hears a sound above a threshold volume.
- MIDI note trigger – sending a MIDI signal at the chosen moment.
- Hitting a foot pedal when ready.

When you have finished recording your sample, ALWAYS check the result by pressing the "Enter" or "Play" buttons on the sampler's front panel, or by playing a note on the keyboard. Remember to hold the note long enough to hear the entire length of your sample.

2. Normalization and Scaling

Once you have recorded your sample, there are many ways in which the sounds can be corrected, edited and generally messed around.

NORMALIZATION is useful if you have a sound that has been sampled too quietly, or a group of related sounds that have been sampled at different levels. It can be used to raise these levels to give the best possible signal-to-noise ratio. Similarly, SCALING can raise the overall level of a group of samples by a predetermined amount.

3. Truncation

Invariably you won't want to use all of the sound you have just sampled. TRUNCATION is a way of trimming the beginning and ending of a sample, leaving you with only the sounds you want to use.

It's always best to start sampling just before the beginning of your chosen sound and continue until the sound has completely stopped. In this way you won't clip the start or cut off any ambience or reverb at the end. The resulting sample can then be truncated to give only the required length. Another reason for doing this is that it save critical memory.

Many modern samplers allow you to control the size of the soundwave image on front panel screen by using ZOOM commands. One method of editing – known as the "rough cut" – starts with the screen zoomed out as far as possible, giving an overall picture of the whole sample. Move the start point up to roughly close to the beginning and move the end point back to roughly after the end of the image of the soundwave. With the extraneous bits roughly edited away, hit the "cut" button. This permanently removes the unwanted top and tail bits. Now zoom in a level and repeat the process. You can continue this until the editing is perfect.

4. Looping

The technique of repeating the whole sample (or specific sections of a sample) is called LOOPING. This is very useful for creating musical patterns that can be repeated over and over again – such as drum loops – or for sustaining the middle section of an instrument sample. For example, consider the sound of a violin string played with a bow. The bow first strikes the string producing a very short ATTACK TRANSIENT. This is followed by a longer steady sound as the player drags the bow across the string. The sound ends when the player lifts the bow from the string, but there is still the sound of the violin body resonating, producing a natural decay to the sound. If we sample this note and then loop the sustained middle section that follows the attack, then when the sample is played back using a keyboard, the attack will sound only when we hit the key. This will be followed by the sustained section which will sound for as long as we hold

down the key. When we release the key, the natural decay of the violin will sound. There you have it – a perfect string sample.

5. Multisampling

Creating a sampled version of a complete instrument – such as a piano, acoustic guitar or string section – is an exacting, time-consuming business which requires the use of a technique known as MULTISAMPLING. This involves taking a large number of samples across the whole range of the source instrument – at least two or three per octave would be typical. For a realistic effect this has to be done to minimize the unnatural sound of a sample being played back above or below its natural pitch.

If you sample someone singing a note and then play back the sample one octave higher, it will sound NOTHING LIKE that person actually singing that note one octave higher. This is because when you play back the sample one octave higher, you are playing the sample twice as fast and for half as long as the original.

Why should this be? Let's look at an example. If your sample is one second long at its original pitch, and has been sampled at a rate of 48,000 individual samples per second, when you play it back one octave higher the sampler will have to play all of those 48,000 samples in half a second in order to double the pitch. Similarly, if you play the sample back one octave lower it will take TWICE as long to HALF the pitch.

Ideally, every individual note of the source instrument should be sampled, looped and assigned to each note across the keyboard. As every note on a piano sounds different depending on how hard it is struck, many samples may be needed for each note to get an accurate sound. Fortunately, there are many CD-ROMs of sampled pianos available where the hard work has already been done for you. Sampling, you see, can be a time-consuming process.

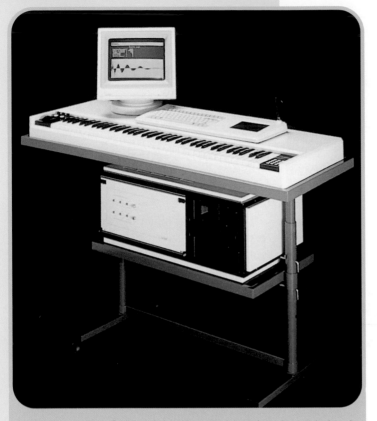

Sampling began with the Fairlight, which could record and manipulate a few seconds of sound.

7. Reverse

You can also play your samples backwards. Some sounds, such as violins and flutes, are quite similar when played back in either direction. Most, however, will be radically different. An endless supply of interesting effects can be achieved by reversing some of the most unlikely samples. Note: if you want to play a sample forwards and backwards at the same time, it will be necessary to copy the sample and edit each one separately.

8. Software Editors and Graphic Displays

As you can see, there is a lot of complex information involved in editing samples. This means that it can be difficult to view everything you need to see on your sampler's tiny built-in LCD display screen. This has led some manufacturers to produce editing software that can be used by connecting the sampler to your computer.

When deciding which sampler to buy, you should check out what editing software is available and find out whether it's compatible with your computer. Most communicate using a standard SCSI interface, which provides fast transfer of samples to and from the computer.

Many third-party sample editors are available, such as Alchemy for the Apple Macintosh. Some MIDI/audio sequencers such as Mark Of The Unicorn's Digital Performer can support many samplers from within the program.

6. Time Stretching and Compression

This is a standard technique for overcoming the consequences of playing samples back at different pitches. When you time-stretch a sample, your instrument will calculate new samples so that you can change the pitch without changing the length of the sample, or change its length without changing the pitch. Many modern samplers and MIDI/audio sequencers can do this automatically. It's really useful for combining samples of different tempos or keys.

Stretching or compressing a sample should be performed with care, though: heavy jumps in tempo or pitch may produce results that vary dramatically in quality.

Organizing Samples

Once you have a collection of related samples, you need to organize them into programs so that you can assign them to your MIDI keyboard. Different manufacturers have different terms for the various parts of their samplers' architecture, but they all work in essentially the same way. Let's take a look at them from the lowest level upwards:

1. Sample

Also known as a VOICE. We've already looked at this area in enough detail for now.

Time Bandit software has the ability to manipulate the length of a single sample in time.

2. Keygroup

A collection of samples. Sometimes also called VOICE ASSIGNMENT.

This is an area of the keyboard – and this can be any number of notes – across which the selected sample will sound. Each keygroup can (usually) contain up to four different samples. Each different sample in a keygroup can be programmed to play back depending on the velocity with which the note is struck.

When you place a sample in a keygroup, you have to select the pitch and MIDI note number you want it to play. Samplers usually default to Middle C (MIDI note value "C3") when you first record a sample, but you can change this parameter

Play New1 Deep Soul Sample L

Time Bandit

Loop   Write Sample

beforehand if you know the actual pitch. When you assign the sample to a keygroup, you can edit the pitch to place it on the correct note on the keyboard. If your samples are made at the default setting (C3) then you will have to tune them up or down depending on the interval between C3 and the correct pitch – if you don't, they won't play back at the correct pitch.

3. Program

A collection of keygroups, usually on a single MIDI channel. When the keygroups contain multisamples any treatments, effects, MIDI channel or output assignments are likely to be the same for all keygroups within the program.

When a program contains drum and percussion sounds, you'll usually want to play them all via the same MIDI channel, but assign them to separate outputs so they can be routed to their own channels on an external mixing desk.

Keygroups can overlap so that sounds can be CROSSFADED to morph into one another, or stacked to allow for the creation of VELOCITY CROSSFADES. All the usual synthesizer-type treatments, such as volume and filter envelopes, filter cut-off and resonance, modulation and other effects are applied in this mode.

4. Multi or Performance

Finally, programs can be grouped into MULTI or PERFORMANCE mode. Multi mode usually contains between 16 and 128 Programs. This is very useful when you want to load up a set of instruments quickly for use with a MIDI sequencer. It only takes seconds to create a new multi, allowing you, for example, to load a drum kit on MIDI channel 1, a bass on channel 2, piano on channel 3, strings on channel 4, organ on channel 5, and so forth. In no time you'll have a ready prepared set of basic sounds with which to start recording into your sequencer. If your creative juices are flowing, you can have the basis of a song programmed in minutes.

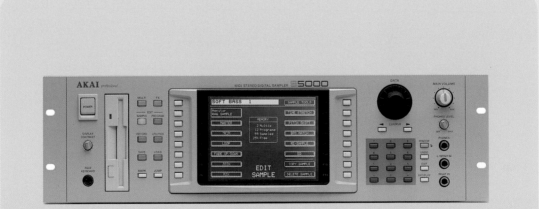

The Akai S5000 is the more sophisticated big brother of the benchmark S1000 model.

Sampling Tips

The hippy cowboy from Mars, Beck combines traditional performance with modern sampling.

Now let's look at some ideas for making your sampling more creative and efficient. You never know, it might even save you a fortune.

Finding Sounds

Your samples will only ever be as good as your sources. Someday, some way, you have to find good samples. The primary source for a lot of dance music is old records. If you're a DJ and have a decent collection then this won't be a problem – you'll have the records and you'll know them well enough to find good bits quickly. If you haven't got the records, then the second best option is to invite a DJ over to your studio.

As a third option, many sample collections are available to buy. Most are far too expensive to sensibly spend your money on, but a bit of co-operation between friends can solve the problem. As the whole point of sampling CDs is to load them into your sampler, it makes sense for two people to buy one disc – after it's loaded into your sampler, you don't really need the CD anymore.

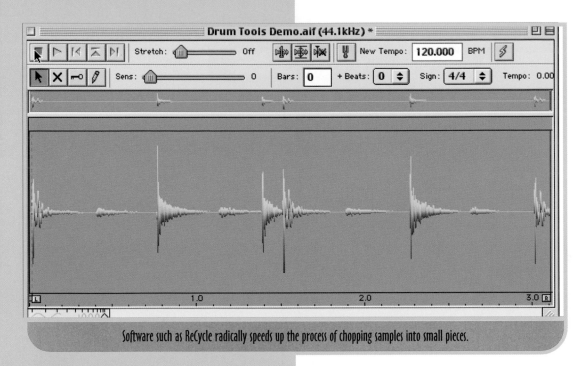

Drum Tools Demo.aif (44.1kHz) *

Stretch: ▭ Off New Tempo: 120.000 BPM

Sens: ▭ 0 Bars: 0 + Beats: 0 ⇕ Sign: 4/4 ⇕ Tempo: 0.00

1.0 2.0 3.0

Software such as ReCycle radically speeds up the process of chopping samples into small pieces.

It's worth mentioning that few people are aware of just how many records with great samples they already own. Even fewer are aware of how many brilliant samples used on big hits have been acquired from the naffest of records. If you can open your mind and think laterally, then those old and embarrassing records might be worth another listen. Try to think in terms of "snapshots". Listen to each drum sound and each drum fill as if it were a single moment of music rather than a part of, say, a Wombles record. Long and sustained sounds, such as a violin note or a choir singing, can be transformed into something very different when used as a looped sample. The possibilities are endless: metal rock snare drums from the 1970s will often fit with machine drums or claps; a twangy guitar lick from the lamest Sonny & Cher record might sound really funky on its own.

It's also important to distinguish between sampled sounds and sampled loops. If you hear a drum that you like on a record and decide to sample it, will you use just the one drum hit, or the whole drum pattern? It's always possible to sample a section and edit just one single strike of the drum. It may also be possible to use more, but how much more? Try to think in terms of beats. Will you try to edit and use two beats of the drum pattern? Four beats? Eight beats? As long as the drum remains in isolation, without any unwanted music on top, then

The Chemical Brothers – a couple of digital geeks.

it can be used. The famous James Brown "Funky Drummer" loop is only four beats long and yet numerous records have used the whole four-beat pattern as the basis for their ENTIRE drum track. Sometimes a better result can be had from using just part of a pattern, or by starting from an unconventional point, perhaps on a half-beat.

If you're choosing and sampling only single hits of drums, then the possibilities for mixing and matching are endless. A bass drum from John Bonham with a snare drum from Steely Dan and a hi-hat from a drum machine might be just the combination you need. Don't forget that drum machines themselves can be sampled for use with other sounds, as can synthesizers – a neat way of "stealing" your friends' new equipment.

Can it be sampled? That is the question. If it can be heard in isolation, even just for one brief moment, then the answer is YES. Obviously, it can be sampled even if there are other sounds, but the background noise or music that comes with it might make it difficult to use. But you can't win if you don't play. The bottom line is EXPERIMENT AND THEN EXPERIMENT SOME MORE. Many great things have already been created with samplers and there's plenty more to come. Try experimenting with strange tunings, tone filters, time-stretching, resonance filters, and whatever else next month's new toy can do to your sound.

Beefing-up Drum Samples

It may often be the case that a sampled drum loop works in every way – it sounds good and clean, fits the groove of the song, and has crisp separation of drums – while at the same time not being

quite powerful enough for a modern record. One solution is to bolster the loop with your own library of drum sounds. This requires careful analysis of the way the drum loop is made up. It really is a matter of manually reproducing the loop on a MIDI sequencer using strong sampled drum sounds, but for it to work properly the loop must be matched precisely. The benefits can be spectacular. If, for example, a new bass drum is programmed to "sit" just beneath the loop's bass drum, then the loop should sound much the same only

Jazzy B, head honcho of Brit samplists Soul II Soul.

with a bit of extra "kick". You can take this further by using equalization (EQ or tone controls) to alter the characteristics of the supporting sounds.

This technique works equally well for sampled bass lines, percussion and numerous other synthesizer sounds.

Groovy Software

If you like to work with drum loops, and the whole process of sampling seems a little tedious when you want to get a track grooving quickly, then software such as Recycle is the answer. This clever program can import audio from a CD, chop it up into individual samples, and then automatically create a program for you with the samples in separate keygroups. Recycle will do so much of the boring work for you – it may even accidentally invent brilliance for you.

The program is a essentially a computer extension of your sampler. It takes a look at the soundwave of your sample and cuts it at identifiable TRANSIENTS – each new loud sound, which in most cases will be a useful division of the beat. For example, it could chop the four-beat "Funky Drummer" loop into 16 pieces. The pieces are then copied back into the sampler, played back in the correct order, AND with exactly the same feel and groove as the original. In this way, you will never be tied to a certain tempo or key of a sample. Even if your entire drum track comes from another record, you can still make the song faster or slower as you wish, but always keeping the drum groove and feel of the old song in tact.

Creating a Sample Library

The creation of a personal sample library can be either a wonderful tool or a slave chain of misery around your neck. It's important either to keep your library short and sweet or, if it's lengthy, well-documented for quick access. The last thing any musician wants to do in a recording session is to sit listening to three hours of "crack... slam... bang... boom... " in search of a beloved old snare sample. The winner is not the guy who can provide the most choice, but the guy who has the winning sound before the vibe of the session has been killed stone dead.

Many sample libraries are stored only on DAT tapes. It's an efficient system and it's non-discriminatory – you can quickly and easily record the sound into any manufacturer's sampler. DAT tapes are long lasting and reliable and it's relatively quick to fast-forward up to the correct "ID" number. Of course, you could carry your library on discs, ready to load and play, but this could be problem if your friend/programmer/employer hasn't got the same kind of sampler.

James Brown has been sampled more times than most of us have had hot dinners.

Using Existing Samples

TO PAY OR NOT TO PAY? THAT IS THE QUESTION. If you make use of a sample from an old record then legally the copyright owner of that music is entitled to some kind of compensation.

So what do we do? Here's a bold answer: sample first, ask questions later. If in doubt, it's probably best to start by doing nothing. That may not necessarily be the safest approach, though.

If you really are very concerned about safety, then undoubtedly the thing to do is hire a lawyer whenever doubt arises. This is advice that holds true for all areas of life. After all, if your neighbour parks his car in front of your house what do you do? You call a lawyer... of course, nobody actually behaves this way in reality, and nor need

DJs are the rock stars of today.

you. The point is that your BEST BET – the way to get the best odds on winning the most for the least amount of expenditure – is to wait and see if it really is necessary.

For most people affected by this decision, the course of events is usually as follows:

1. You decide to use a sample from an old record for your new song.

2. It sounds great and you start to wonder about your legal position.

3. 500 "white labels" 12-inch singles are pressed up are sent out to DJs.

4. You earn a bit from it – maybe enough to recoup what you have already spent.

From this point, however, the story may now go in one of three directions:

The hype slows down and then stops: no further copies are pressed. In this scenario, you are happy not to have paid out for lawyer's fees and a sample clearance fee. The sample is forgotten about and you are soon busy with your next project, albeit a bit more flush than you would have been if you'd paid out.

Or...

The hype carries into a second pressing: you are able to fund the next single. Again, you are very glad to have kept the extra cash. The total amount you earned in this scenario is less than ten thousand pounds and no one is going to consider suing you to recover a percentage of such a relatively small sum.

Or...

The Motown studio, home of numerous widely sampled classics.

The record explodes, you are signed up by a major label and life is sweet. Maybe now you might regret that you didn't act safely. With your profile on the rise, the likelihood of threats of legal action against you increases. NOW is the time to hire a lawyer. However, since the vast majority of cases are settled before trial, your chances of ending up in court are still small. You will probability pay a slightly higher sum to the "injured party" (the sampled artist) than you would have done had you taken the "safety" route. And your legal fees won't be much more than they would have been in the first place.

This may sound quite mercenary – unethical, even – but it's certainly not intended to encourage you to break the law. Think about it for a moment, though: who actually gets hurt? The injured party may lose out on the tiny sum that should have been paid up front. But this small sum would not have been trivial to you. To be honest, would you even bother to experiment with these samples if they were costing you a few hundred pounds each time? Of course not. What struggling artist has that kind of money to risk on every attempted production? Many artists are making these records with hopes only of earning little more than that themselves. Of course, if success strikes you will be happy to come to a reasonable agreement about the royalty split and everyone will be happy, right?

Of course, this only applies to those artists who make records privately, without a prior recording agreement. If you are in a deal or have a contract of some kind with a publisher, record company, or anyone else who may be affected, then you will do well to keep them informed and listen to their advice in these matters. Especially if they offer to stump up for all the costs incurred.

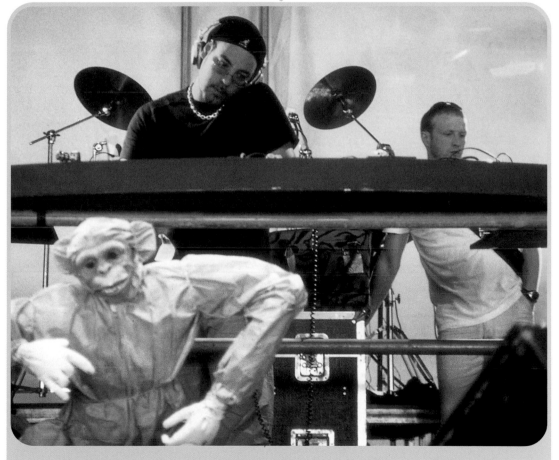

New York DJ Roger Sanchez managed to hover near the top of the DJ/producer/remixer pack throughout the 1990s.

CHAPTER 4

MIXING
DESKS

Before digital audio, a recording studio was only ever as good as its mixing desk.

The audio mixing desk – also known as a CONSOLE (posh), BOARD (cool), PULT (Teutonic), or SONIC BLENDER (Sci-Fi/Star Trek/post-modern) – has traditionally been the centrepiece of every recording studio. It provides the conduit for all audio routing and basic sound treatments.

The live room at The Strong Room Studios, London.

Although the control room of a professional recording studio may look like the bridge of the *Starship Enterprise*, dominated by a huge mixing console adorned with hundreds of knobs, switches and lights, the desk is actually quite simple to understand when broken down into its component parts.

The first important concept to tackle is the signal flow. The audio signals come into the desk at the top and flow down vertically. They are first "treated" or "processed" in the vertical channel and then flow out in a horizontal direction (don't worry, this will all make sense shortly).

All mixing desks, from the tiny to the mammoth, contain two main sections. These are the INPUT CHANNELS and the MASTER SECTION.

input Channels

Even budget desk producer Mackie has got in on future digital sounds

A mixing desk's basic job is to combine audio signals. This means that at least two input channels are required, otherwise there's nothing to mix. In practice, desks usually have from four to in excess of one hundred input channels. A typical small-studio mixing desk will have 24. Let's take a look at a typical input channel in more detail:

1. Microphone and Line Inputs

Any mixing desk needs to be able to handle input signals from a wide range of devices. The MICROPHONE/LINE SWITCHES and TRIM CONTROLS are used to normalize the various signals so they can work alongside one another on the desk. Some desks also have a CHANNEL-FLIP switch on this section for switching to TAPE PLAYBACK mode from any connected multi-track tape machine.

2. EQ

EQ is an abbreviation for EQUALIZATION. This is a term that comes from the telecommunications industry, and was used to describe boosting a phone-line signal to correct or "equalize" losses in level over long-distance telephone lines. The various EQ controls on a typical mixing desk provide a more sophisticated and effective type of tone control than would be available on any electric guitar amp or home stereo amp. (An in-depth look at EQ can be found on page 67.)

3. Auxiliary Controls

This useful and versatile collection of controls can be used to "siphon-off" some of the input signal to send to external effects boxes (or to a musicians' headphones for monitoring). You can never have too many auxiliaries on your desk – three is an absolutely bare minimum.

Auxiliaries can be switched between PRE-FADE or POST-FADE modes. Pre-fade means that the level set by the auxiliary control is independent of the channel fader so that when you pull it down the auxiliary level is unaffected. When in post-fade mode, pulling down the channel fader will proportionately decrease the auxiliary level. The post-fade mode is the normal setting when using effects – pre-fade is generally used for foldback monitoring (*see Chapter 7*) or special effect set-ups (*see Chapter 5*).

4. Groups

The GROUP buttons are used for routing the input signal to a different part of the mixing desk via what are termed MIX BUSSES. Desks are usually described in terms of their channel capabilities. For example, 24-8-2 describes a desk with 24 input channels, 8 mix busses, and 2 master (stereo) outputs. The buss outputs of this desk could be connected to an 8-track tape recorder (or doubled-up for a 16-track or tripled-up for a 24-track).

5. Panning

This control "pot" (which is an abbreviation of "potentiometer", and refers to any rotary knob on the desk) enables a signal to be placed in the stereo panorama. Here it can be "panned" left, right, or anywhere in between.

6. Mute and Solo Buttons

When the MUTE button is activated no sound can be heard from that channel. The SOLO button does the reverse, muting all the other channels so that only that channel can be heard.

7. Channel Fader

This is the long vertical slider control found at the bottom of each input channel. It controls the final level of the input signal, and all its post-fade auxiliary signals, before it is sent to the master section or the mix busses.

Other Input Channels

Many modern desks have a combination of input channels designed for different purposes. For example, signals from synthesizers or samplers don't necessarily need microphone pre-amps, and may not even need EQ or effects. These can be connected to a simple stereo input with one volume fader controlling both channels. This saves space and, above all, cost. After all, there's no point in paying for stuff that you don't need.

Don't worry, it's all much simpler than it looks.

Master *Section*

As its name suggests, the MASTER SECTION is the command module of the desk. All of the inputs and outputs are ultimately routed through this part of the desk.

1. The Master Faders

A pair of mono faders (or sometimes a single stereo fader) controls the main output level going out to the master two-track (stereo) recorder.

2. Effects/Auxiliary Returns

These control the level and (sometimes) EQ of the signal coming back from any connected external effects units.

3. Selector Switches

This set of controls is used to select inputs from the master two-track recorder or other sound sources such as connected CD players and cassette decks.

4. Monitors

A variety of monitoring facilities can be controlled from the master section of the desk. You will invariably find pots for controlling the level of the signal sent to the control room monitors and to the studio TALKBACK system, which enables the engineer to communicate with musicians outside of the control room. On multi-buss desks, you'll also find a set of group channels. These look rather like cut-down input channels. The outputs from these groups can be sent directly to individual tracks on a multi-track recorder.

A Solid State Logic (SSL) desk is a brilliant mixing tool... if you can afford it.

Cutting the groove – old-style vinyl still plays a major role in modern dance music.

Automation

With the advent of multi-track tape recorders with 24 tracks and more, mixing became a far more complex process. At first, an "all-hands-on-deck" approach was necessary, with the producer, engineer, assistant engineer and various members of the band all handling small sections of the mixing desk – switching channels in and out, riding faders, switching in effects. A near-perfect mix would often be ruined by someone missing a cue, leaving only one option: to start again. Very difficult mixes were often done in sections that were subsequently edited together using a razor blade and splicing tape – Queen's epic "Bohemian Rhapsody" is a prime example of this approach.

80 channels of lean, mean automated mixing muscle machine crammed into a single SSL frame.

mixing consoles, is Solid State Logic. By the middle of the 1980s, an SSL desk had become the ultimate "must-have" for any serious professional studio. But being at the cutting-edge of technology didn't come cheap: a new SSL would have (and still does) cost hundreds of thousands of pounds, with prices escalating towards the million-pound mark for a large-format, top-of-the-range model.

The Perfect Sound?

The high-end desks we've been describing are so expensive because they are built to order and use custom-designed computers to run them. They have the highest quality components and a comprehensive installation and back-up service. What you get is full automation of all desk functions, motorized faders which can read and write and be used to update mix information at any time, and a top quality sound. There are, however, different types of "top quality sound". Engineers, producers and musicians will all talk at great length about their personal sound preferences – you can be sure that no single desk will ever satisfy all of them. The truth is that no matter how much you pay, there's no such thing as THE PERFECT SOUND.

Do I Need Automation?

Of course, this talk is all well and good after a few international hit albums, but for the average small studio owner, taking possession of an SSL desk is a pipe dream. But if you want to make your own automated mixes is it really necessary to spend a vast fortune? Let's just consider for a moment what desk automation actually entails:

The first attempts at mix automation came in the late 1970s. These systems were difficult to use, expensive and notoriously unreliable, employing technology similar to that found in analogue synthesizers. Eventually, digital control proved to be the answer. One pioneering company whose name has become synonymous with automated desk automation actually entails:

- A means of recording data, fader movements, muting, effects sends, and then playing it back.
- The ability to edit and constantly update data.
- Synchronizing so that it's perfectly in time with your music.

Sounds like the perfect job for a MIDI sequencer.

Digital SOUND

In the 1980s, automation took off with the birth of the first fully digital mixing desks. One of the most significant models was the revolutionary 8-channel Yamaha DMP-7. It featured motorized faders, two DIGITAL SIGNAL PROCESSORS (DSPs) providing built-in reverb and other effects, and full automation controlled internally via snapshots or by using an external MIDI sequencer. The price was around £3,000. This was made possible only because the DMP-7 was fully digital. The input signals were converted into digital data and all the internal processing – EQ, dynamics, routing and effects – was performed digitally. The data was only converted back to an analogue signal at the desk outputs. You could save a "snapshot" of all the desk settings at any given moment, name it and recall it at any time in the future. What's more, several DMP-7s could be chained together to provide more channels.

Over the past decade the market for digital desks has proliferated, with outstanding models such as the Yamaha 02/R, 03/D and 01/V, the Mackie D8B and Soundcraft 328 all appearing for less than £5,000.

But although these "budget" digital desks may seem too good to be true, they do have certain drawbacks. The sound quality is generally considered inferior to analogue desks of a similar price, especially in their EQ and effects capabilities. Furthermore, they rarely have insert points to connect to external processors.

Virtual Desks

When MIDI sequencing programs were first written for personal computers in the early 1980s, they were designed in such a way that would make their functionality and appearance familiar to musicians and sound engineers. The software was operated using transport controls that looked like those of a tape recorder. In addition to this, a virtual mixing desk consisting of faders and pan pots was included to control the volume and positioning of attached MIDI sound modules. These worked by sending out MIDI data to the connected modules on individual MIDI channels.

As personal computers became more powerful it became possible to record and edit audio on the computer. Although these early designs were limited they provided very powerful editing facilities that were impossible to achieve using traditional methods. Pioneers in this field were Digidesign's Sound Tools and Deck, both of which were designed to run on an Apple Macintosh computer. Features from both of these programs were later combined to make up the ProTools system – far and away the most popular computer-based digital audio recording and editing system used by audio professionals.

The ProTools 24MIX system now provides recording, editing and mixing for 64 separate audio tracks at 24-bit resolution. But when it comes to mix automation, Pro Tools is the undisputed king, even outperforming the best high-end hardware consoles.

The modern age of digital recording and mixing means that today's biggest recording studios are not necessarily the best. In fact, the power of a top 1980s studio can now be fitted into a single laptop computer – including the desk, recorder, effects... and even some of the instruments.

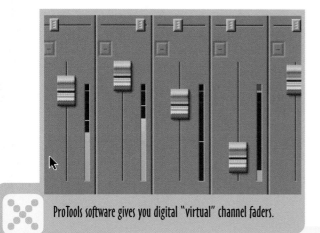

ProTools software gives you digital "virtual" channel faders.

Throughout the late 1990s, the manufacturers of all of the major MIDI sequencer software packages also began to incorporate facilities for digitally recording audio tracks into their systems. Without fail, each of them now incorporates a virtual mixer that provided all the typical desk facilities including EQ, inserts, sends, panning and faders, together with multiple busses, groups and masters. Their sonic capabilities can be further enhanced by the ever-expanding range of PLUG-IN programs which can provide a variety of high-quality digital effects.

The long-term future of mixing desks is undoubtedly in the virtual arena. For the meantime, however, all types of desks can provide top-quality and workable options. Perhaps the eternal answer to "what desk?" will always be "horses for courses".

The Logic Software's virtual mixer page can handle as many digitally recorded tracks as your computer's "RAM" memory will allow. Each track can be named for its sound, with individual EQ, inserts and effects. Internal "bouncing" or sub-mixing of tracks can be performed quickly and simply.

New Edit View Options

Audio

No Selection

EQ		EQ		EQ		EQ
ParEQ	ON	ParEQ	ON	HiShlf	ON	HighC
970	Hz	970	Hz	9400	Hz	7000
0.0	dB	0.0	dB	0.0	dB	
0.63	(Q)	0.63	(Q)			
ParEQ	ON	ParEQ	ON	ParEQ	ON	ParEQ
970	Hz	970	Hz	970	Hz	970
0.0	dB	0.0	dB	0.0	dB	0.0
0.63	(Q)	0.63	(Q)	0.63	(Q)	0.63
ParEQ	ON	ParEQ	ON	ParEQ	ON	ParEQ
970	Hz	970	Hz	970	Hz	970
0.0	dB	0.0	dB	0.0	dB	0.0
0.63	(Q)	0.63	(Q)	0.63	(Q)	0.63
ParEQ	ON	ParEQ	ON	LoShlf	ON	LowCut
970	Hz	970	Hz	100	Hz	80
0.0	dB	0.0	dB	0.0	dB	
0.63	(Q)	0.63	(Q)			
Inserts		Inserts		Inserts		Insert
Sends		Sends		Sends		Sends
I/O		I/O		I/O		I/O
In ADAT 1		In ADAT 2		In ADAT 3		In ADA
Out 1-2		Out 1-2		Out 1-2		Out 1-
Track 1		Track 2		Track 3		Track

90	90	90	9

M S	M S	M S	M
O REC	REC	O REC	RE
KIK	SNARE	HAT	RACK

| EQ | EQ | EQ | EQ |
| Thru | Thru | Thru | Thru |

EQ	EQ	EQ	EQ	EQ	EQ	EQ	EQ	EQ	EQ
hCu ON	HighC ON	ParEQ ON	ParEQ ON	HiShlf ON	HighCu ON	HighCu ON	HiShlf ON	ParEQ ON	HiShlf ON
00 Hz	000 Hz	970 Hz	970 Hz	9400 Hz	7000 Hz	7000 Hz	9400 Hz	970 Hz	9400 Hz
		0.0 dB	0.0 dB	0.0 dB			0.0 dB	0.0 dB	0.0 dB
		0.63 (Q)	0.63 (Q)					0.63 (Q)	
EQ ON	ParEQ ON	ParEQ ON	ParEQ ON	ParEQ ON	ParEQ ON	ParEQ ON	ParEQ ON	ParEQ ON	ParEQ ON
Hz	970 Hz	970 Hz	970 Hz	970 Hz	970 Hz	970 Hz	970 Hz	970 Hz	970 Hz
dB	0.0 dB	0.0 dB	0.0 dB	0.0 dB	0.0 dB	0.0 dB	0.0 dB	0.0 dB	0.0 dB
(Q)	0.63 (Q)	0.63 (Q)	0.63 (Q)	0.63 (Q)	0.63 (Q)	0.63 (Q)	0.63 (Q)	0.63 (Q)	0.63 (Q)
EQ ON	ParEQ ON	ParEQ ON	ParEQ ON	ParEQ ON	ParEQ ON	ParEQ ON	ParEQ ON	ParEQ ON	ParEQ ON
Hz	970 Hz	970 Hz	970 Hz	970 Hz	970 Hz	970 Hz	970 Hz	970 Hz	970 Hz
dB	0.0 dB	0.0 dB	0.0 dB	0.0 dB	0.0 dB	0.0 dB	0.0 dB	0.0 dB	0.0 dB
(Q)	0.63 (Q)	0.63 (Q)	0.63 (Q)	0.63 (Q)	0.63 (Q)	0.63 (Q)	0.63 (Q)	0.63 (Q)	0.63 (Q)
Cut ON	LowCut ON	ParEQ ON	ParEQ ON	LowCut ON	LowCut ON	LowCut ON	LoShlf ON	ParEQ ON	LoShlf ON
Hz	380 Hz	970 Hz	970 Hz	380 Hz	380 Hz	380 Hz	100 Hz	970 Hz	100 Hz
		0.0 dB	0.0 dB				0.0 dB	0.0 dB	0.0 dB
		0.63 (Q)	0.63 (Q)					0.63 (Q)	
serts	Inserts	Inserts	Inserts	Inserts	Inserts	Inserts	Inserts	Inserts	Inserts
ends	Sends	Sends	Sends	Sends	Sends	Sends	Sends	Sends	Sends
I/O	I/O	I/O	I/O	I/O	I/O	I/O	I/O	I/O	I/O
DAT 5	In ADAT 6	In ADAT 7	In ADAT 8	Input 1	Input 2	In S/P 1	In S/P 2	In ADAT 1	In ADAT 2
t 1-2	Out 1-2	Out 1-2	Out 1-2	Out 1-2	Out 1-2	Out 1-2	Out 1-2	Out 1-2	Out 1-2
ack 5	Track 6	Track 7	Track 8	Track 9	Track 10	Track 11	Track 12	Track 13	Track 14
90	90	90	90	90	90	90	90	90	90
M S	M S	M S	M S	M S	M S	M S	M S	M S	M S
REC	REC	O REC	REC	O REC	REC	O REC	REC	O REC	REC
CK 2	FLOOR	O/H L	O/H R	BASS	LOW TOM	LOW TOM 2	TENOR SAX	Audio13	CONGA L
EQ	EQ	EQ							
ru	Thru	Thru							

CHAPTER 5

FAIRY DU
AND MAG
EFFECTS

The Red Valve virtual guitar amplifier from Steinberg.

You've already had a glimpse into the world of effects. Now let's take a deeper look at this increasingly significant area of recording.

Although there are many different effects used in the modern recording world, they can all be placed into two general categories: those which simply change a sound without adding any new

components, and those which add something extra to the basic sound.

The first category of effects can be thought of as operating on the sound much like a water filter works on the tap: it may remove certain impurities,

thereby exaggerating the pure qualities of the resulting water. But it brings nothing of its own into the picture. Effects that work in this way are rather like a screen through which a sound must pass. The effects are "inserted" into the signal path of the chosen channel on the mixing desk, the sound in the channel "passes through" the effect and emerges from the other side sounding in some way different. Effects in this category include EQ, COMPRESSION and NOISE GATING.

The second category could almost be thought of as actual sound sources, because they all add something that didn't exist before the effect was plugged in. Since these effects add another sound to the overall mix, they require their own input channels on the mixing desk. As you are sure to discover in no time, no desk is ever big enough, so manufacturers get around this problem by creating dedicated RETURN channels for these kinds of effects (*see page 56*). In essence, these inputs are just like the normal fader channels on the desk, but usually consist of just a simple volume control.

Every external effect unit has input and output sockets (or pairs of sockets for stereo effects). The input socket on the effect must be connected to the AUX SEND socket on the mixing desk; the output socket should be connected to the EFFECT RETURN input on the mixing desk.

Most modern units can produce a wide array of effects, and will generate some kind of sound as soon as they are powered up and plugged in. As always, experimentation is the key. Start by scrolling through the presets, listening to each new effect as it happens.

Equalization

Equalization (EQ) is by far the most common effect used in recording and mixing. Most sounds in a production will usually be subjected to some sort of EQ. Indeed, its use is so common that few producers or engineers would even consider it an effect – they would more likely think of it as a standard procedure. As you've already seen in Chapter 4, all mixing desks whatever their quality will offer some sort of EQ on every input channel.

Plug-in EQ can produce very detailed filtering.

Logic's "FAT EQ" is a powerful (if a bit crude) plug-in.

EQ In Practice

Equalization is a necessity in modern mixing. This is primarily because our ears have become accustomed to different sounds from those that occur naturally. Because radical EQ has been used in pop music since its earliest days our perception has reached point where a snare drum without that extra "crack" or a piano without extra "treble" is likely to sound dull and boring to most listeners.

In essence, EQ is the addition to or removal of certain frequencies of a given

FilterBank plug-in EQ.

becomes 400 Hz; "C4" has a frequency of 800 Hz; "C5" is 1,600 Hz; "C6" is 3,200 Hz, "C7" is 6,400 Hz, and "C8" (a very high note on the piano) has a frequency of 12,800 Hz.

Without needing to remember these numbers, you must at least memorize the three golden rules of equalization:

THE MAIN BASS FREQUENCY IS 100 HZ

THE MAIN MID-RANGE FREQUENCY IS 1 KHZ

THE MAIN TREBLE FREQUENCY IS 10 KHZ

Different EQs

There are several different kinds of EQ. The simplest form is referred to as CUT-AND-BOOST. Here you are given up to four fixed frequencies each of which can be boosted or cut as desired. This is what is usually found on a mixing desk and is the main workhorse of the music mixing business.

PARAMETRIC EQ allows you to choose the frequencies before cutting or boosting them. Rather than being given the fixed choices of standard cut-and-boost systems, you set your own choice of frequency. With parametric EQ the process has two basic steps. Begin by setting the FREQUENCY CHOICE control (which usually takes the form of a rotary control) and then try cutting and boosting to see if the result sounds good. If that doesn't work for you, try a different frequency and then cut and boost again. You can also approach this process from the opposite direction by setting the cut and boost and then turning the frequency control. This creates the "filter sweep" effect heard on a lot of dance music.

A third type of EQ known as FULLY PARAMETRIC EQ is more complex and is mainly found in professional studios. It allows the cutting or boosting of extremely precise frequencies or ranges of frequencies.

sound. The most common example is BASS and TREBLE. Frequencies (sound waves) are measured in terms of cycles per second (known as HERTZ and abbreviated as "Hz"). A healthy young human ear can hear all of the frequencies between 20 Hz and 20,000 Hz (20 kHz). The lowest pitches in music, such as a bass drum or a bass note on a piano, will be at the bottom of the scale, below 100 Hz; the higher pitches – such as cymbals, the top notes on the piano, flutes or piccolos – will be among the upper frequencies, above 10 kHz.

How Frequencies Work

Somewhat confusingly, the middle distance between 20 Hz and 20 kHz is NOT 10,000 Hz. This is because sounds do not increase steadily but are exponential or logarithmic in nature. Without getting too "Einstein" about it, the most important thing to remember is that the frequency of a pitch doubles with each octave above it. Roughly speaking, if the lowest note on the piano (designated as "C1") has a frequency of 100 Hz, then the note 12 notes higher – one octave above that note (C2") – will have a frequency of 200 Hz. This process escalates continuously in the same way: after a further octave ("C3"), the frequency

Compression and Gating

Ever notice that when you put a classical CD on the stereo you never seem to be able to set the volume properly? And that the soft bits always need to be turned up to be heard, and the loudest bits make the neighbours complain? And yet whatever volume you set a pop CD, every bit of can be easily heard. Why should that be?

This is the secret. While the classical buffs developed the CD precisely to accommodate the huge dynamic range (the difference between the quietest and loudest bits), the bare truth is that in pop music there is no "loud" and no "soft". A whisper is always turned up loud enough to be heard over the drummer, while the screams are turned down enough not to blow the speakers. How is this done? Simple. When the singer whispers, you push up the fader on the microphone channel; when he screams, you pull it down again. The trouble, however, comes with being able to react quickly enough to a singer's ever-changing volume. This is where we bring in a very handy device called the COMPRESSOR.

Controlling Dynamics

In music, the term DYNAMICS simply means loud and soft. And that's what compression is all about: controlling dynamics. Before 1955, the only thing a recording engineer could do was to "ride" the fader up and down, trying to counter-act the volume of the singer. Believe it or not, both he and the singer would watch a giant "VU" meter (a level indicator) with the aim of trying to keep the needle near the middle. That was the original form of compression.

Things have become more sophisticated since then. Electronic compressors track the signal and "kick in" when the level goes over a preset THRESHOLD. In this way, the dynamic range of a singer or instrument can be reduced. An excellent example of a wide dynamic can be heard on any Nirvana album. The singer, Kurt

Virtual dynamic effects have the added benefit of programmability and automation.

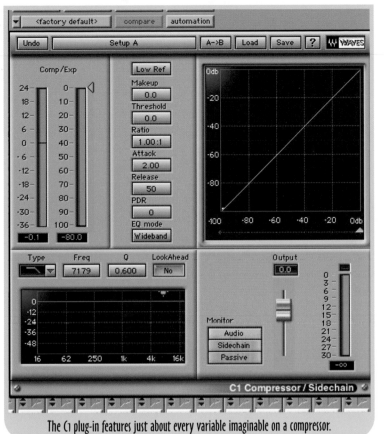

The C1 plug-in features just about every variable imaginable on a compressor.

the ratio is the amount by which the gain is reduced. The threshold should be set just above the point on the meter where things start to get a bit loud, and you should always start with the gentlest compression ratio of 2:1. As the ratio increases you will notice the sound of the compressor lowering the volume. A ratio of 10:1 and above is quite severe and apparent, and the top setting of "infinity" is so severe that is known not as compression but LIMITING. This sets a volume level that the machine will simply not allow the sound to go above. You can hear this effect on the radio when a DJ lets out a sudden shout. The noise he makes must be prevented from exceeding the maximum volume (or else your speakers would blow) – it's the radio station's limiter that prevents this happening. Listen carefully when the DJ screams and you can hear his voice sounding "squeezed".

Compression is SO important. You really should spend plenty of time experimenting with the different thresholds and ratios. Once you have a good grasp of what these two parameters can do, try playing with the other controls on your compressor. ATTACK and RELEASE governs the way in which the compression kicks in once it passes the threshold, and how it switches out when it's brought below the threshold. More often than not, a fast attack time and a slow release time is used, but you will find that different settings allow more severe compression to become less noticeable.

Cobain, had a neat formula where verses were very quiet and the choruses very loud. In spite of this, the different sections of the songs still manage to sound about the same in volume: the verses are quite clear, even on the car radio at 60 mph with the window open, while the heavy duty choruses pose no threat to your speakers. This is a vastly reduced dynamic range. This is compression.

Compressor Controls

Although a compressor may have many different types of control there are only two that you really need to understand: THRESHOLD and RATIO. The threshold is the point where the volume will start to be turned down (often called GAIN REDUCTION) and

Compression is a vital factor in achieving that ever-elusive "radio sound". As such, plenty of practice with this effect will improve the overall sound of your music.

Noise Gates

GATING is the opposite of compression. Instead of shrinking the dynamic range of a sound, this effect increases it. It isn't usually intended to make a musical difference, but rather to increase the distance between the musical and background noises like hiss and rumble. For this reason it's also sometimes known as EXPANSION.

Once again, the two main variable parameters are threshold and ratio. The threshold is the point at which the gate will begin to turn down the volume, and the ratio is the rate at which the volume will be reduced. The threshold should be set just above the softest musical sound and the ratio is almost always set very high. When the background noise is "gated away" the apparent distance between the loudest point (the singer's screaming) and the softest point (the background hiss when the music stops) is greatly increased.

The other functions on a noise gate are likely to be the same as those found on a compressor. The attack determines how quickly the gate will react and is usually set to the minimum (or fastest) time, while the release determines how quickly the gate will reopen after closing and is generally set quite near the minimum (or fastest) time. Different settings will help to mask the effect and avoid any clicks that may occur with severe gating.

Many noise gates have an extra socket labelled EXTERNAL KEY which can be very useful as a special effect. Normally the gate will close and open according to the level of the signal. This is called the INTERNAL mode and will be used in 99 percent of applications. By changing the noise gate to external key mode, the gate may be closed and opened according to the level provided by an external sound, while still effecting the original signal. In this way, you could make a lead vocal "stutter" (or TRANSFORM to use DJ-speak) as though it was being turned on and off in time with the beat (which it would be doing if it were "externally keyed" from the drum channel). It can be a finicky trick to set up, and may take hours to perfect, but the effect can be exciting and startling. Once again, lengthy experimentation is the only way forward.

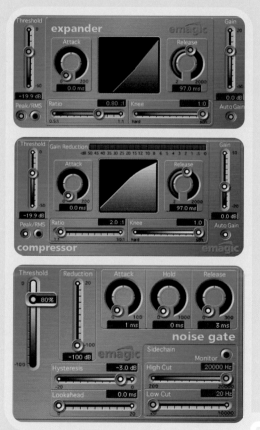

Three handy ones from E-magic: a powerful noise gate/expander; a simple compressor, and an easy-to-use noise gate.

Delay

Just about all other effects known to man are based on the simple idea of a delaying a signal. This is done using a DELAY BOX (or DELAY LINE), a unit which takes any input sound, holds onto it for a predefined time, and then spits it out the other side for you to mix in with the original "dry" sound. If the delayed sound and the dry sound are mixed together at about the same volume, magical things can be heard, although the specific nature of the effect will depend on the length of the delay between the two signals.

All delays are measured in milliseconds (ms), which are thousandths of a second. The shortest delay possible on most machines is 1 ms. When a sound is delayed by such a small amount and mixed evenly with the dry sound, the result is an effect called PHASING. This popular psychedelic effect can be created by any delay of up to about 8 ms, and is greatly enhanced if the delay time is adjusted while being heard. Such a movement of the delay time is called MODULATION.

When the delay on the sound is increased to between 10 ms and 15 ms, the effect is of a lightly different nature and is called FLANGING. Strictly speaking, the delay time must be modulating before the sound is truly flanging.

Delay times of 18 ms to 25 ms create a much-loved effect known as CHORUSING. This effect also requires modulation of the delay time and is often said to resemble a sort of "underwater" sound. With delay times of 30-60 ms, the effect becomes known as ARTIFICIAL (or AUTOMATIC) DOUBLE TRACKING (ADT) or DOUBLING. When used on a lead vocal, it sounds as if the singer has performed a second almost identical take in order to strengthen the sound of the voice.

When the delay time reaches around 80 ms the situation changes. Suddenly the delay can be heard as being distinct from the dry sound. From 80 ms to around 120 ms, the delayed sound creates a ricochet effect. This type of delay, known as SLAPBACK, has been used by everyone from Nashville country singers to likes of John Lennon.

When the delay time is above 130 ms, most people begin to hear the time between the dry and the delay as being a distinct echo. Delays of this length and beyond must be used carefully – they can wreak havoc with the sound and rhythm of a beat. Experimenting with delays that are exactly in time with a song's tempo can yield interesting results. It is also very common to use delays that repeat in a sort of loop, gradually getting softer with each repetition. This is called FEEDBACK and is usually available within the digital delay preset controls.

Of course, this way of looking at effects is not apparent when you return from the music store and take a first glimpse at your new digital delay box. Manufacturers provide endless presets which you can simply "dial up", listen to and modify. And this a good a starting point for experimentation.

So now you know why all these lovely effects can so easily be put in one small and cheap box: they're really all just slight variations on the same theme.

PRO TIP: When using digital delay of 20-40 ms on a lead vocal, adding a touch of modulation will vary the delay time and help bring the sound to life.

Reverb

The sound of reverberation is not a special effect at all. It is, in fact, the most common noise you ever hear. It is simply the sound made when a noise bounces off a surface. When you speak in a small room, the sound of your voice reaches your ear directly from your mouth. However, your voice will also be bouncing off the walls (albeit very quickly) and the ricochets reach your ear slightly after the direct sound. This effect is almost unnoticeable in your sitting room, but you are well acquainted with the same effect as it occurs in a large concert hall. In those caverns, the sound of someone's voice comes into your ear not only directly from his mouth but also from the ceiling and the walls and the backs of 10,000 metal chairs. The rainstorm of slightly delayed reflections, that hits your ear in rapid succession, creates the "spray" of sound that follows the original sound of the speaker's voice. In a large auditorium, this effect can last for many seconds after a word has been uttered, thereby forcing the speaker to talk very slowly if he intends to be understood. This spray is called REVERBERATION and it ranges from the long trail of hollow ringing that follows every sound made in Wembley Arena to the very short, imperceptible reflection of your own voice which takes place when you lock yourself in your broom closet.

The only places that are entirely devoid of natural reverb are a large fields on a perfectly still day or when a person speaks or sings closely and directly into your ear. Thus, if you present a person's recorded voice without adding some sort of reverb, the sound may seem more "effected" than the same voice with reverb added. Music studios are frequently designed so as to be acoustically "dead" with no naturally occurring reverb. This is in order to allow for you to apply your own choice of electronic reverb. Remember, though, any reverb recorded onto the tape along with the voice cannot be later removed: you'll be stuck with it forever.

Electronic reverb units allow you to simulate different types of surroundings. A short reverb of less than one second indicates a small room and can be very effective for sharp, tight sounds, such as fast-tempo drums. Middle-length reverbs of about 1.2 to 2 seconds are handy for most general uses. Long reverbs of more than 2.2 seconds are generally reserved for use in slow-tempo ballads or for special effects in other types of music. Reverbs of more than 4.5 seconds are very rarely used in pop music.

The EMT Reverb Plate was the world's first artificial echo chamber and is still in frequent use today.

EMT

The TrueVerb plug-in does a decent digital plate reverb.

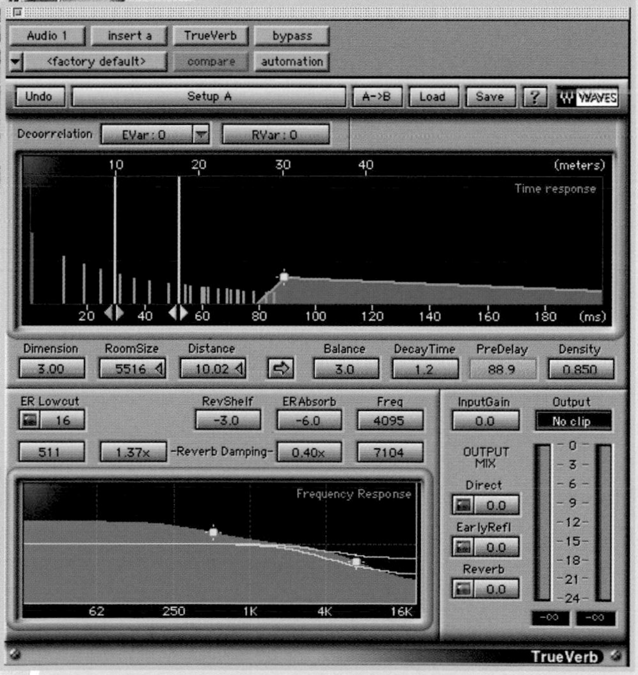

Audio 1 | insert a | TrueVerb | bypass
<factory default> | compare | automation

Undo | Setup A | A->B | Load | Save | ? | WAVES

Decorrelation | EVar: 0 | RVar: 0

10 · 20 · 30 · 40 (meters)
Time response

20 · 40 · 60 · 80 · 100 · 120 · 140 · 160 · 180 (ms)

Dimension	RoomSize	Distance		Balance	DecayTime	PreDelay	Density
3.00	5516	10.02	⇨	3.0	1.2	88 9	0.850

ER Lowcut | RevShelf | ERAbsorb | Freq | InputGain | Output
16 | -3.0 | -6.0 | 4095 | 0.0 | No clip

OUTPUT MIX

511 | 1.37x | —Reverb Damping— | 0.40x | 7104

Direct
0.0

EarlyRefl
0.0

Reverb
0.0

Frequency Response

62 · 250 · 1K · 4K · 16K

0
-3
-6
-9
-12
-15
-18
-21
-24
-∞ · -∞

TrueVerb

Reverberation
EMT 1
for stereo EMT 140

Virtual Effects

Plug-ins open over the top of the on-screen virtual mixing desk.

The term PLUG-IN generally refers to a tiny computer program that adds additional functionality to a larger one. For instance, web browsers can be enhanced by the addition of plug-ins so they can play real-time audio and video clips over the Internet. This approach has been enthusiastically embraced by the designers of computer audio processing software.

The first commercially successful audio plug-ins were written for Digidesign's ProTools. This was made possible because the system used custom-designed add-on hardware that contained Digital Signal Processor (DSP) chips capable of providing the necessary power boost to deal with the

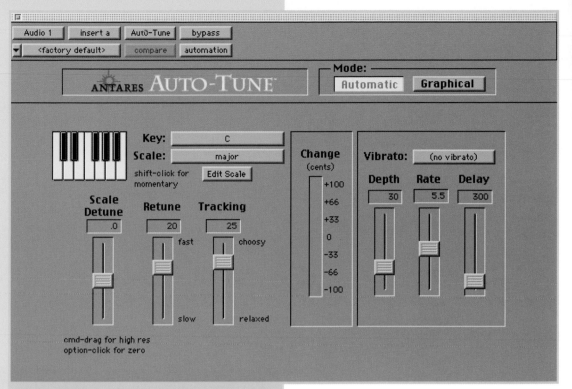

Prominent on Cher's worldwide hit "Life After Love", this little rascal turns a lousy singer into a virtually good one.

intensive real-time calculations needed for reverb or complex delays.

As computers became faster and equipped with more and more memory, it became possible do away with dedicated DSP FARMS (collections of linked processor chips) and let the computer's main processor run the plug-ins. This was the approach taken by Steinberg's Cubase VST. This was a bold attempt to create a virtual recording studio on a computer, complete with virtual effects racks... and even a virtual leather armrest on the virtual mixing desk.

This technology continues to progress at a rapid rate with traditional effects, equalization and dynamics processing being emulated by computer software. Many manufacturers of audio hardware such as Lexicon, Focusrite and Drawmer have produced plug-in versions of their hardware units. Others have reversed this trend, developing hardware boxes based on successful plug-ins – Antares Autotune (*see above*) and Line 6's Amp Farm guitar amplifier simulator (*see left*) are two good examples.

Just as the use of traditional outboard effects boxes is a matter of personal taste, plug-in favourites vary from person to person. Reverb is generally considered to be the most difficult effect to realize in this way, and some would say that there is no plug-in available that can approach the capabilities of the Lexicon 960L reverb unit. (Although with this model costing £13,000 this is no great surprise.) Broadly speaking, the best approach is to use plug-ins only for audio treatments that are difficult to achieve by

Strange effects emanate from the digital distortion of the Bitcrusher.

other methods – unless, of course, you particularly like the sound of certain favourites.

Compatibility

A word of warning: plug-ins are not universally compatible, but are written for a particular format – usually based around the manufacturer's own audio software. Examples of this are TDM (Digidesign), VST (Steinberg), RTAS, Audiosuite and Premier. Some designers, such as Waves, use a "shell" program from which their plug-in collection can run. In this way, only the shell needs to be re-written for each format.

As well as the standard effects described above, VST has a rapidly expanding base of other plug-ins from which you can choose. These include:

• Those that are used for tuning correction, pitch-shifting and time-stretching, making it possible to correct tuning and accuracy, change tempo without changing the key and vice versa, such as Autotune, Pure Pitch, Pitch Doctor, Pitch'N'Time.

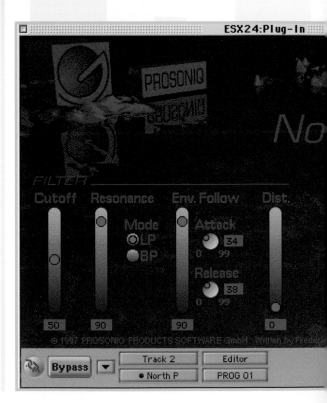

The E- Magic Spectral Gate takes boring sounds to another world and back again.

The North Pole is one of the original plug-ins — and it's still among the best. Startling filter and resonance effects can easily be created by this wonderful toy.

"sound warpers" (vocoder-style sounds which impress the characteristics of one sound onto another).

- The fastest-growing area of development is the ever-growing range of virtual synths and samplers that can be controlled by an external MIDI keyboard and totally integrated into the audio sequencer environment. Again, some of these are software emulations of classic instruments, such as the MiniMoog, Prophet 5 or PPG Wave 2.3. Others are interesting new designs such as the Koblo series and the Unity DS-1 software sampler.

Using Plug-ins

Plug-ins can be described as being either REAL TIME or OFF-LINE.

- Software imitations of guitar amplifiers, speaker cabinets, microphones and expensive, hard-to-find vintage valve gear, such as Amp Farm, Antares Mic Modeler and the Bomb Factory.
- "Bit crushers" – software for dirtying-up sound by converting the files to lower bit-resolution, creating "Lo-Fi" sounds) and

Real-time plug-ins can be accessed by the inserts and sends on a virtual mixing desk in exactly the same way as their hardware counterparts. The great advantage is that every parameter can be automated. You can insert them into the virtual mixer's input channels or into a group/auxiliary channel which acts as an effects return treating the proportion of signal being sent from the input

Nothing beats MondoMod's 360-degree phase manipulation (above). The Ultrapitch (right) aims to improve on the idea of the harmonizer.

E-Magic's virtual sampler brings the power of digital sampling to the computer environment.

channel. These real-time plug-ins do not affect the original audio file, and can therefore be changed at any time.

Off-line plug-ins differ in that they are used to permanently alter the original audio file. The main advantage is that a less powerful computer can be used to play back the audio files. This also means that a song can be played back on a different system exactly as it was recorded, without having the original plug-in present.

Although the purchase price of plug-in effects may seem to be quite high, audio/sequencer software manufacturers always include a comprehensive set as a part of their packages. There are also many widely available fully featured demos which "time-out" (self-destruct) after a period of time, giving you the opportunity to try before you buy. The Internet is an especially good source here.

The classic Sequential Circuits Prophet 5 synthesizer, recreated as a cyberspace plug-in.

CHAPTER 6
THE FINA MIX

The art of mixing is in the details. With hundreds of fiddly bits to check and recheck, some sort of system and organization is vital. As with driving a car, no one would ever be able to do the job properly if they had to look for the accelerator or the brake before pushing it down. Likewise, when mixing it pays to put things in their place every day. It's a bad idea to use the same sound sources for the same instruments day after day – a better solution is to simply move the leads at the back of the desk. It only takes five minutes at the beginning of a mix session to change around inputs until your "usual system" is in place.

Two weird dudes — David Byrne of Talking Heads (left) and Brian Eno (right) have each made considerable contributions to the progress and art of music production.

where To Begin

A common approach when starting a final mix is to begin at Channel 1 with all the drum sounds – bass drum, snare drum, hi-hat, tom 1, tom 2, floor tom, cymbals – and then bass guitar, guitars, keyboards, all the backing vocals and finally the lead vocal. It's also a good idea to plug your effect auxiliary sends in a regular way – reverbs on sends 1 and 2, and delays on sends 3 and 4, for example – and to confine all the effects' auxiliary returns to the desk's specified effects input channels. Whatever you choose, stick with it. Put some white tape across the bottom of the desk channels and mark the instrument names on it in a thick, coloured marker (but make sure the tape doesn't leave nasty, sticky stuff when it comes off).

80s DJ/Remixer Jellybean Benitez

If your desk has enough input channels, put only one sound in each channel. This will enable you to give each one separate EQ, effects, volume and panning. If your desk doesn't have enough channels (or if a particular mix has more sounds than there are channels), be sensible about what you double up. For example, if two sounds are both "thin and toppy" (such as a hi-hat and a ride cymbal) and they are likely to need roughly the same effects and panning, there's no harm in putting them in the same channel and adjusting their relative volumes at the sound source (the sampler or beat box).

You also need to organize your body so you are comfortable and can see the whole desk, the sequencer screen and – this is important – the DAT recorder's level meters (or whatever type of machine you choose for mastering). The input to the DAT machine is last thing your music sees before you commit it to eternity, so you should never allow more than a few minutes to pass without checking that those levels look healthy. Your chair should ideally be on wheels. This will encourage you, having made adjustments, to return to the midpoint between the two speakers. It's important to keep checking the stereo picture and to keep checking the sound at different volumes.

Speaking of volumes, one of the least understood switches on any home stereo is the one called "loudness". Everyone knows that it sounds better when engaged, but no one really knows why. The answer lies in psychology and anatomy. The human ear performs best when it listens to louder sounds. When the ear is trying to hear quiet sounds, the survival instinct kicks in. The brain and ear assume that the most important sound is the human voice (in order to seek food or sex) so, at low levels, they zoom in on the range of the voice – frequencies of around 1 kHz. The telecommunications industry knows this very well which is why telephones are EQ-ed to bring up the mid-range frequencies. Similarly, hi-fi companies know that people listen most often to relatively quiet volumes – which the ear will hear with exaggerated mid-range. The "loudness" switch tries to counter-act this by boosting the low and high frequencies when the volume is low,

thereby (theoretically) levelling the sound and restoring the "true" effect of the music.

All of this is merely to point out how important it is for you to change the "monitor" volume (of your speakers) regularly. It's always a good idea to have a system: perhaps keep a clock by the desk and split the hour into loud, medium, soft, and very soft clock-radio volumes. Ideally, you should analyze each volume on a variety of speakers. It's always a surprise when you hear how different a mix sounds on a different set of speakers. For the icing on the cake, make a cassette of your mix-in-progress and listen to it in the car, in the kitchen, or at a friend's house. By hearing your mixes in different environments you get an idea of how others will hear your music. The beauty of this is that if you are still in the middle of the mix then you can go home and fix any of those annoying problems.

A quicker test for your mix-in-progress is to hear it through a doorway from a different room. Play the mix on the control room speakers at whatever volume and simply walk into the next room or corridor. It's amazing how a little distance can freshen one's perspective.

Early-90s samplists PM Dawn successfully managed to recycle old fluff into new funk.

Levels

The most important technical aspect of any mix is keeping a firm control of the levels. The overall level coming out of the mixing desk must be correct, averaging near to "0", and without any surges off the scale. The level going into the DAT recorder must ALSO be right, averaging near the top of the meter without any surges. This is no mean feat which even the best mixers sometimes get wrong. If the levels are too high you will probably have an unusable final mix; if the levels are too low you will probably have a noisy or poor-quality final mix.

The most common problem for beginners could be referred to as "faderitis". This is when, during the course of a mixing session, some of the faders get pushed all the way to the top. It usually happens because the master faders were set too low at the beginning of the session, so the mixer tries to create power and volume by pushing up the individual channel faders. THIS IS A DEAD-END ROAD – THE ONLY WAY BACK IS TO PULL DOWN ALL THE FADERS AND START FROM SCRATCH.

To avoid this problem you need to train yourself into good habits. Try this system:

1. Remember to start with the monitor level (the volume) as loud as if you were listening to a CD.

2. Set the master fader to just above "0" – maybe "+1" or "+2".

3. Decide what the loudest level sound in the final mix is likely to be. This may sound impossible, but it's usually easy. For dance music, it's ALWAYS the bass drum. For most other kinds of music it's generally the lead vocal. Whatever it is, roughly EQ and compress this sound first, setting the fader at a level so that the desk output meters just below "0". Now set the input levels on the DAT recorder so that they are just below the desk meters.

4. Build the rest of the mix around the main sound. This doesn't mean you must leave the main sound on all the time, but rather that you must compare all subsequent sounds to the main sound to set the rough levels.

5. Try not to move the main sound's fader – even if this means putting a piece of sticky tape over it to keep it still. To take it out of the mix always use the channel mute switch instead.

6. Don't pull down the master fader at all, UNLESS YOU ABSOLUTELY HAVE TO. If the mix levels look good except for one or two short surges, you might consider taking it down to "0" or even "–1" or "–2". But if you need to pull it down much further to keep the levels within control, then you've gone too far and will have no option but to pull all the individual channel faders down and start again.

Obviously this is just a rough system to establish some initial control over the levels, but you should find that this approach creates good habits for producing clean and powerful-sounding.

The Third Dimension

A good mix is more than just a combination of loud and soft sounds. The picture needs to be three-dimensional, so experiment with the left/right of panning, and the front/back of reverbs and delays.

There's nothing quite like the smooth glide of a real fader.

Panning seems a lot easier than it is. It clearly doesn't take much skill to move sounds laterally by turning a pan pot left or right. The secret is in the OVERALL PICTURE. It's important that a mix should not be too heavily weighted to one side. Try to think of panning sounds in pairs to even out the mass. If a drum track has two hi-hats try panning one to the left and the other to the right. If two snare drums are used, or two rhythm guitars, pan them opposite to maintain a balance. If a particularly strong sound works well when panned hard-left, try slowly panning it to hard-right at a key moment during the final mix.

Get into the habit of regularly checking the sound of the mix in mono. Most desks have a stereo/mono switch for this purpose. This will ensure that your record still sounds good on the clock-radio or in the car. A "mono-listen" can also reveal things about the stereo mix that you had previously missed. Don't forget that some members of your listening audience may never get to hear the record while sitting in the middle of the speakers, so pay attention to how things sound when heard from only one side.

Using a very short constant delay on a sound can make it seem to exist "behind" the other sounds. Rhythm guitars and pianos often get a delay of 30 ms or 50 ms set slightly softer than the dry signal. This has the effect of "pushing them back" into the mix. This delayed sound could even be panned at "9 o'clock" and the dry sound to "3 o'clock" to exaggerate the effect.

Some mixers use visualization to help with their productions. They may imagine the act on stage and "place" the sounds accordingly. The drums are panned in the middle and given plenty of mid-length reverb (1 to 2 seconds) to place them at the back of the stage. The bass player stands in the middle with the drummer, but with less and shorter reverb. The guitars and keyboards have similar reverbs and short delays and are panned left and right stage. The backing vocals are at the back and off to the right with plenty of reverb. The lead vocal is loudest (to keep it at the front) and with plenty of reverb, but this reverb has a "pre-delay" to stop him from being swamped.

Whatever you do, though, don't forget to keep the channels allocated to true stereo sounds panned to extreme left and extreme right.

Understanding Frequency

A good mix is often like a good painting – it needs a variety of colour. In music, the colours could be thought of as the different frequencies, so a good mixer will always ensure that there is an even spread. Remember that the bottom of the spectrum – 40 Hz up to about 300 Hz – should come from the bass drum, the bass guitar and the low piano notes. So make sure that thin sounds like hi-hats don't have any extraneous "boom". As a rough guide, EQ your low sounds so they have less "highs" and your high sounds so they have less "lows". If your desk EQ offers it, try the high pass filter (or rumble-filter, or low-cut switch) on the thin, high sounds. If you don't actually write these details down on paper, you should at least keep a picture in your mind of the distribution of your mix.

Don't forget to experiment with cutting frequencies as well as boosting them. EQ can sometimes affect the apparent level of a sound more than the actual fader position, so you may need to adjust the fader after EQ-ing a sound.

EQ and Effects

Effects will also react to changes in EQ on the dry sound. A dark, bassy sound will usually create an atmospheric and subtle reverb, whereas a bright

40 Hz – 300 Hz	Kick drum, bass synthesizer, low piano.
300 Hz – 700 Hz	Cello, low guitar, piano chords, drums (depth), bass guitar (clarity).
700 Hz – 1.5 kHz	Synthesizer lead line, male vocals (body), violins, lead guitar, drums (power).
1.5 kHz – 4 kHz	Vocals (power), drums (crack), kick drum (click), general clarity.
4 kHz – 9 kHz	Drums and cymbals (presence), general sharpness and presence.
9 kHz – 19 kHz	Vocals (breath and air), cymbals (sheen), general "zing".

EQ on the sound will instantly make the reverb stand out and take up far more space. While the nature of a sound's EQ and reverb will most often live happily together, it is possible to keep them separate. One method – called a CHANNEL SPLIT – is to use a Y-adaptor lead. This can simultaneously connect one sound to two different channels, allowing you to have one channel for the EQ and level and another channel from which to send the raw sound into a reverb (or other effect). With this method it is necessary to ensure that the second channel is not putting a duplicate of the dry sound in your mix – the "doubling-up" of an identical sound in a mix may do very strange things, such as making it louder or even cancelling it out completely. You can avoid this by either disengaging the "mix" button on the second channel or by keeping the fader all the way down and using the reverb auxiliary send in pre-fade mode (*see page 55*).

Delay Trick

Another good use for this channel splitting trick is to send the second channel to a very long delay (perhaps more than 200 ms). Again, ensure that the dry sound is not doubling-up in your mix and send the post-fade sound to the delay. With the "delay FX" channel you can ride the fader up during key moments, for example, to get a delayed repeat of just one word or note: the rest of the time the fader should be kept all the way down. This is the way that lead vocal tracks are improved with an "echo" delay on only the last word of each line: "Do it baby, (baby, baby), Do it right, (right, right)". In this example, the delay channel fader must be pushed up ONLY during the moments when the vocalist sings "baby" and "right" – the rest of the time the fader is kept down.

Frequency ranges for the different instruments.

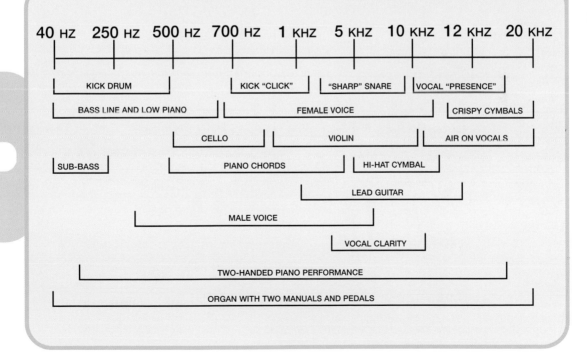

Layering

Like a good cake, a good mix usually consists of different layers. You need plenty of the chewy spongy stuff for texture. And you CERTAINLY need plenty of chocolate frosting. The best ones will have several cleverly alternating layers. You should try to approach a production in this way. With few exceptions, too many guitars spoil the broth. Too many drums will be a mess without velvety reverb between the layers. Variety is surely the right spice.

The Perfect Production?

When it comes to the issue of what constitutes a good production, one thing is certain: THERE IS NO SIMPLE FORMULA.

The range of good production techniques is very wide indeed. Some records work well with hundreds of sounds in them. The great American producer Phil Spector perfected this kitchen sink approach in his legendary "wall of sound"

From the German industrial city of Düsseldorf, Kraftwerk have been a massive influence on the evolution of dance music.

productions. These epic productions had a traditional "backline" (drums, bass and guitar), a full orchestra (including all the frills like chimes and kettle drums), plenty of keyboards (piano, electric piano, organ, h a r p s i c h o r d , glockenspiel, mellotron), plenty of backing vocals (full choirs), not to mention the lead vocalists who often had enormous voices to compete with these armies and to add to the sheer size.

Equally, some records work well with very little instrumentation. Singers like Suzanne Vega and Bobby McFerrin have produced perfect records with nothing but their own voice. And Kraftwerk pioneered a stripped-down minimalism which has influenced numerous dance artists over the past two decades. Producers such as Brian Eno and Daniel Lanois place great emphasis on the "ambient" quality that comes from space. There are, of course, many thousands of soloists who have never even contemplated adding more sounds to their records.

George Martin (left). Many have called him the "Fifth Beatle".

The Producer as Artist

One common thread through these excellent records is the way they have been produced. Sometimes it's in the orchestration and sometimes it's in the mixing. Orchestration – or deciding which instruments should play which notes at what time – has always played a key part of large productions. Phil Spector and George Martin (the producer of the Beatles' greatest recordings) are among the finest practitioners of the art: songs such as "You've Lost That Lovin' Feeling", or anything from the *Sgt. Pepper's Lonely Hearts Club Band* album provide better lessons in orchestration than any book or tuition. Just listen to the textures and pay careful attention to the way the instruments weave in and out, and what happens to your heart when they do.

Regardless of the size of a production, nothing will sound right in a bad mix. Those enormous sixties productions required careful use of reverbs to allow so many layers to taste good together, just as Suzanne Vega's *a cappella* records require the perfect reverbs (or a perfect dryness). Heavy layering will also require efficient use of the entire stereo space (or mono space for a different vibe altogether) so give extra thought to subtle panning in big productions.

Remixing

What is a remix? The only sure thing is that it is not the first mix done of a song. Beyond that point, it depends largely on who you talk to. Before 1975, the term simply referred to a second attempt at a mix of a song – usually because the first attempt failed. From the late sixties, reggae producers such as Lee "Scratch" Perry, King Tubby and Cool Herc experimented with alternate, longer versions of their own productions and invented many of the (then strange) sounds which are common today.

In the 1970s, disco producers such as Giorgio Moroder and Nile Rodgers began to translate the idea of alternate commercial versions of singles. These early 12" singles differed from the original only in length and they were longer only because they were edited using a razor blade. Soon afterwards, the "disco" market grew to a size where record companies found that they could make substantially more money by commissioning disco 12-inch versions for general release. These hired "remixers" were the original artists and producers themselves, until the companies realized that they could sell more

The Dreem Teem: 21st century DJs.

copies to clubbers if the clubbers made the records. By 1981, with the explosion of the rap scene to fuel the dance music fires, record producers were hiring club DJs to help them with their remixes. It wasn't long before the inmates took over the asylum.

The original eighties DJ remix kings, notably Jellybean Benitez, Junior Vasquez and Arthur Baker, relied heavily on help from established engineers and producers. They always remixed the song directly from the original master tapes (there was no other way) and there was a feeling that the remix shouldn't be so different from the original as to be unrecognizable. And after all, there wasn't *that* much anyone could do to an existing song. They tended to run the tapes a little faster for a faster tempo and, maybe, get a funkier drummer to replay the drums. With very few exceptions, remixing was like offering a T-shirt to boost sales.

The Modern Way

By 1990, it was a whole new ball game. The introduction of affordable sampling (and hard-disk recording) meant that old songs could be manipulated without

An inspired DJ can melt all the world's music into a single night.

relying on the original master tapes. Tempos could be radically altered and whole backing tracks could be re-recorded. Even the key could be changed. Now there was no limit – anyone could attempt to rework a song without anyone's permission and without access to the master tapes. Without any technical boundaries, even the most un-funky song could be transformed into a dance hit. Every producer, every artist, every engineer, and every record company wanted a piece of this new pie.

At some point in the last decade, the idea peaked as a marketing concept. The remix actually became more important than the original version and the word became the source of confusion that it is today.

There's no doubt that just about any record made is capable of becoming – and should be tried or at least contemplated as – a remix. Mostly this means a dance remix, but alternate versions of any record will always be a selling point. More versions means more markets means more sales. Welcome to the world of remixing.

Approaching a Remix

The crucial starting point when you attempt a remix of anyone's record (even your own) should be to ask yourself one simple question: "What am I trying to do here?" While it may be possible to create a remix from the ground up – with no plan – these usually end up sounding directionless and (worse still) gratuitous. Furthermore, a record company will begin by trying to pigeon-hole the genre (read "the market"), so you might as well play the game. As long as you are already finished with the main version of the song, what have you got to lose?

When it comes to remixing (among most other things) record companies generally don't like surprises. Therefore, most successful remixers are hired specifically for the fact that the record company is expecting a certain type of sound from them. So before starting a remix, it's

probably a good idea to confirm exactly what is required: how many versions? How many styles? How long each remix should be. The Top 40 chart rules are quite strict about the number of minutes that a single can offer, so even the best remix will have to be cut if it exceeds that limit.

These days, a remixer is expected to create an entirely new production from scratch using just the hooks or other identifying sounds. The down side is that it's extremely unlikely that the remixer will get either the producer credit or a royalty. Most of us are working for the wage on the day.

That's your lot. Of course, at the top of the tree this may be serious cash – maybe $50,000 for a couple of days work for the star US DJs – but the vast majority of remixers earn very little indeed. For them, the prize is a day in the sun, a chance to show off their stuff to the Big Boys. In a word, ACCESS.

Big-time producer William Orbit is best known for his work on Madonna's Ray of Light album.

CHAPTER 7
LIVE RECORD

Although great music can be made without recording live sound, the "machine-only" road is only so long. Somewhere along the line you're going to have to use a microphone. In any case, nothing beats the thrill of a good live performance.

The Legendary Neumann U-47.

If live recording is a rare treat in your studio, the expense of buying a microphone may not be justifiable. In such cases you may be better off by hiring a microphone for those special occasions. Renting the perfect microphone for each job is a privilege for a recording engineer, but is far too expensive if required often.

Don't panic too much when you see the prices of microphones. Many home studios manage with just one good model: one singer, a group of six singers, a saxophone, a three-piece brass section can all be brilliantly recorded with just the one decent microphone.

As we saw in Chapter 1, a microphone creates only a very weak, low-level signal. This is why a microphone has to be connected to the designated "mic" input on the mixing desk. If there is only a single input for microphones and "line level" sources then there will be a "mic/line" switch to tell the desk what kind of level to expect. Indeed, even if there are separate inputs for "mic" and "line", the desk will still have such a switch to tell the desk what to levels to expect when the signal arrives. When set to "line", the channel will expect a louder signal than when set to "mic". So when you plug in your microphone make sure that the "mic/line" switch to "mic".

ING

Changing technology has altered the fundamental way in which music is recorded. Before the birth of digital sampling and the widespread use of synthesizers all music was essentially "live".

Microphones

Microphones come in two general categories: DYNAMIC and CONDENSER. Dynamic microphones are relatively cheap (but can still sound pretty good), can withstand being dropped on the floor and require no external power to make them work; condenser microphones are rather fragile and require their own power supplies, but they inevitably sound much better, even if they can cost a small fortune.

Condenser microphones require a supply of 48 volts of electricity to work. However, this power does not come directly from a power socket, but is sent from the desk to the microphone along the microphone lead. This miraculous invisible supply is

A groovy little collection: (from left-to-right) condenser, dynamic and PZM microphones.

Dynamic Microphones

- Shure SM–57 — This and its twin – the SM-58 – are the most popular microphones in history.
- Sennheiser 421 — A commonly used microphone for drums and electric guitar.
- AKG D–12 — The classic Kick Drum mic.
- Electro Voice RE–20 — Another good model one for kick drums, guitars and low-voiced radio DJs.

Condenser Microphones

- Neumann U–87 — The best all-around microphone ever made; it sounds good on everything.
- Neumann U–47 — An extremely high-quality microphone for voice, acoustic instruments, and soft sounds.
- AKG 451 — A crisp and clean microphone which is ideal for sharp sounds such as cymbals and steel guitars.
- AKG 414 — A classic model for just about everything – a close second to the U–87
- Calrec "Soundfield" — A fidgety and gimmicky microphone that has been known to work magic.
- PZM — Stands for "Pressure Zone Microphone" – a weird, square, flat mic for recording ambient sounds (*see top right*).

Madonna sporting a head-set microphone.

Sheryl Crow displays a fine example of microphone sense.

desk's capabilities before buying or hiring such a model. In truth, it's not the end of the world if your desk can't supply phantom power – 48-volt power supplies cost very little.

Microphone Sense

Always remember to use a high-quality microphone lead, one that's not too long. You should also try not to run it over mains power leads as this can result in additional undesirable buzzing and humming sounds. Don't allow the microphone to get wet or humid and, if your singer is prone to spitting or drooling while at work – protect your investment with a foam POP SHIELD.

It's never a good idea to hold the microphone while singing, so make sure that you have a sturdy stand – preferably one with a counter-weight that can balance the effect of a large microphone. If the stand has three legs, place one leg directly beneath the lateral extension "boom" arm to help prevent the whole thing toppling over. In fact, use whatever materials you have at hand – gaffer tape, heavy books, string tied to the ceiling – to ensure that the microphone does NOT hit the floor with any great impact.

The microphone stand should also be placed sturdily so as to avoid vibration from other sounds. If necessary, you can place the stand on a thick piece of carpet. Alternatively, place the singer on a piece of carpet – this can also be effective in preventing the singer's tapping foot finding its way onto the finished recording.

called PHANTOM POWER. You should be able to find a switch on the desk which needs to be turned on to generate this power. Don't worry about the threat of electrocution here – 48 volts is actually a tiny amount and there is no risk of shock should you touch it. Unfortunately, some cheaper desks do not have a facility for phantom powering, so check your

A standard pop shield protects the microphone and prevents over-enunciated "P", "D", "T", "K" and "B" sounds from creating unpleasant "popping" noises. A satisfactory alternative can easily be made by stretching a nylon stocking over a wire coat hanger opened out into a hoop shape. This can be fixed to the stand directly in front of the microphone in such a way that the vocalist sings "through" the loop.

An ideal studio has the recording room (foreground) isolated from the control room (background). This studio goes one stage further, a glass panel allowing those in either room to maintain visual contact with each other.

make the room silent. A second idea is to record the singer in an isolated room. Ideally you should aim to both, creating a silent and private "recording room".

The area in which you position your desk, speakers and recording gear is called the CONTROL ROOM, while the room where the musicians perform is the RECORDING ROOM.

Any room can be made into an acceptable recording room. The first requirement is that it be made silent for the duration of a session. This may involve expensive insulation on the walls, ceiling and floor, or it could involve setting up a small temporary booth using sticks and blankets and rope hanging from nails in the ceiling. It could also involve using your front room in its normal state, only working at night when the traffic is quiet.

There is no real formula for what makes a suitable recording room. Some people have

Location

When you record a singer, you are also recording all the other sounds in the room where the performance is taking place. In most cases this is not a desirable state of affairs. One solution is to

The industry-standard Beyer DT-100 remains the most popular set of professional headphones ever made.

succeeded in using a bathroom as a vocal booth with no modifications at all, while others have failed after endless effort and expense. At the very least, you should make sure that there is no echo or "ring" in the room. One final word, don't choose the grand ballroom as your recording room as it probably has way too much natural reverberation.

The only other requirement you need from your recording room is that you can run a microphone lead between there and the desk in the control room and still be able to shut the door.

Foldback

If your performer is going to sing in an isolated recording room there has to be some way of allowing him to hear the music on which he is overdubbing. This backing music reaches the singer's headphones via a system known as FOLDBACK. This is so-called because the noise he is making will come down the microphone into the desk and then be folded back to him once again so that he can hear what's going on.

When you first hear the live microphone on the mixing desk, you will probably want to "warm up" the dry sound by "sending" some of the signal to an external reverb unit. As you have already seen in Chapter 4, you can do this by turning up one of the auxiliary send controls – whichever one has a reverb unit attached.

At this point, you must also "send" the sound back to the singer. To do this, choose one of the auxiliary sends as your "foldback send" and connect a lead from its output all the way to an amplifier in the recording room. This need not be a particularly high-quality amplifier – just one that has a headphone socket and a pair of closed-cup headphones. Now the singer can hear his voice in the headphones. To increase the volume of the voice in the headphones, all you have to do is turn up the auxiliary send on the microphone's input channel on the desk. If there is more than one singer or performer in the recording room, you will need to get extra pair of headphones and a SPLITTER BOX to plug them all in.

The secret of live recording engineering is to check out the sound of the foldback headphones before the singer gets to hear it and then to adjust this foldback mix (also known as the "headphone mix" or "cans mix") until the levels are correct. This is a much prized studio art – professional studio singers who encounter a good foldback mix will often employ that recording engineer again.

Recording Vocalists

Recording a solo singer is surprisingly simple to do well. To begin with, the microphone and stand needs to be positioned and the levels need to be set. For a singer, the most obvious position is to place it directly in front of the mouth. Ask the singer to close his eyes and sing as he intends to do on the track. Now check to see if he crouches down or looks upwards or turn sideways, and adjust the microphone's position accordingly. If he dances around too much, you may need to have a brief discussion about "microphone technique" – just try to get him to keep his mouth within a reasonably small area. When working with a singer who moves around a lot, direct the head of the microphone towards his chin rather than his nose. This will help to avoid an overtly nasal sound. Whatever the case may be, study the singer's position for a few minutes until you are satisfied that the sound of the voice is near-directly towards the microphone and is at a distance of two-six inches from the mouth.

If you hear a "pop" sound on the letters "P", "D", "T", "K" or "B", you will need to use a "pop shield" between the mouth and the microphone. You can use a proper version or simply make a hoop from a wire clothes hanger and stretch a pair of tights over the top – there is no audible difference. It can be tricky to arrange the shield so that it sits just in front of the microphone, but most engineers manage with the application of a few pieces of gaffer tape.

Groups of singers often seem to sound better when recorded on a single microphone than when recorded separately. Remember that the microphone is DIRECTIONAL (or if suitably equipped it has been set to the single-direction CARDIOID position) and that all the singers must stand close together and sing with their mouths near to each other and facing the same direction as the mic. Such close grouping will also help the singers to unify their performances, pitch and timing. To accommodate the different voices, groups may need to stand a bit further back from the microphone – perhaps 10 to 20 inches – unless the nature of the music is soft and/or intimate, in which case they should retain a "close" position.

PRO TIP: Always keep the sound of the microphone well compressed, toppy and loud in the vocalist's headphones – singers love nothing more than hearing their own voices sound good.

Brass

The piercing blast of a trumpet requires a high-quality microphone to capture its sound effectively.

A saxophone player is similar to a singer in that he will want the same foldback mix and the same sort of microphone position. Use a slightly greater distance – about 10 inches from the microphone to the mouth of the instrument – but aim directly at it.

Solo trumpets and trombones will need even greater distance – maybe up to three feet, if it's really blaring out – and you may need to switch on the PAD SWITCH if the microphone has one on it. This will make it less sensitive to such a loud sound. Remember that the louder players need to have a lower volume of their own sound in the foldback.

If you record a brass section that comprises three or more pieces, it may be easier to record each player one-at-a-time. However, if the section insists on performing together you can try them all on the same microphone, but you must be quite careful to capture a perfect balance of all the instruments. Furthermore, if they are recorded all on a single track there can be no adjusting the balance later on in the mix. In such situations it's usually a good idea to do a few warm-up takes and then invite the musicians in to check that they are happy with the balance. Brass players themselves tend to be good at picking out and assessing the balance the different instruments.

Guitars

In recent years, electric guitars have become very easy to record. Many players now show up for a session with their own racks of equipment and simply hand you a lead to plug straight in to the desk. These new boxes generally sound great, and in these circumstances no microphones are needed.

If the player wishes to go the traditional route and use his guitar amplifier, the classic approach is to use a cheap dynamic microphone placed in front of the amplifier's loudspeaker – almost touching it. If this doesn't create a good enough sound, try using a different microphone or move it back a few inches at a time until it improves.

Because electric guitar amplifiers tend to be very loud, you may find that, rather than using the foldback system, it's easier for the player to simply use a long lead and sit in the control room while he performs, leaving the amplifier in the recording room with the microphone.

Acoustic guitars are a completely different story. Indeed, they are arguably the most difficult of instruments to record. The answer is to get the best condenser microphone you can lay your hands on and position it six inches away from the guitar's soundhole. This is much easier said than done, since most acoustic guitarists move while they play. To make life easier, choose a chair or a stool that is comfortable for the player. Put some sticky tape on the chair and the floor if necessary to show the player where he must stay. String squeaks can be reduced by putting powder on the strings; excessive plectrum noise can be reduced by moving the microphone further away.

The classic approach to recording a guitar is to place a dynamic microphone in front of the speaker.

Bass Guitar

In most modern studio situations, the electric bass guitar is invariably recorded without the aid of a microphone. Normally the bass is connected to a DIRECT INJECTION BOX (also known as a DI BOX) which is then plugged into the microphone input on the mixing desk. This approach will always work painlessly and sound good.

For a REALLY wild bass sound, try this experiment. Take a hefty professional, power amplifier – at least 150 watts – and simply plug the bass directly into either the left- or the right-hand channel. Now connect the speaker output straight into the mixing desk. Inexplicably, it's the best bass sound known to mankind.

Weather Report's Jaco Pastorius was known for making even the simplest of songs come to life with his innovative bass technique. His chosen weapon was the Fender Jazz electric bass guitar.

Drums and Percussion

A session recording live drums can the Mother Of All Recording Sessions. At least five microphones will be required, as well as a powerful foldback amplifier so that the drummer can hear the other instruments over the clatter of his own playing. You must take great care placing the microphones in such a way as to avoid the calamity of the drummer hitting one very hard with a stick. Since the sounds are all very loud, microphones with pad switches will need them turned on. To begin with, all the pots and faders should be kept quite low in volume. You should also keep the speaker volume down most of the time.

As with all live recording, it's important to listen to the instrument being played in the room with your own ears, before making a few mental notes about what you hear. Does the kick drum flap or boom? Should it be taped up? Is the snare drum tight enough or does it ring too much? Does it need some tape or other dampening? Are the tom-toms tuned properly? Are the cymbals bright enough? Are any of the drums inappropriate for the kit or the song? Should the snare drum really be a different size or depth? Are the heads too new or too worn? Discuss any or all of these points with the drummer and come to an agreement before setting up.

The traditional method of recording drums uses one microphone for each drum except the snare, which uses two. The kick drum microphone (ideally an AKG D-12) is placed inside the drum head. A blanket is usually placed over the kick to help keep the sounds separate. The snare can use a Shure SM-57 coming just above the rim – but pointing away from the drummer – aimed at the centre, and a brighter microphone (perhaps an AKG 451)

The "Funky Drummer" himself, Mr Clyde Stubblefield.

underneath, aimed at the snares. This bottom microphone provides less than half the sound and is mainly there to add "crispness" from the rattling snares. Another bright microphone goes about three inches above the hi-hat on the opposite side to where it's hit. Each tom-tom gets a chunky mic like (an SM-57 will do fine here) pointing downwards at the centre of the drum head (just peeping over the rim). Each cymbal can be given a bright microphone hanging about eight inches above and aimed at the centre of the bell. Finally, a matching pair of good condenser microphones are positioned high above the kit (three feet or more) in a way such that one covers the left-hand side of the kit and the other covers the right-hand side, forming a perfect stereo, ambient "overhead" pair. If the ceiling is not high enough, this overhead pair could be replaced by a "distant" pair, maybe five or ten feet away.

The drum kit provides the ultimate challenge for any recording engineer.

It is, in fact, possible to record a drum kit with three or less microphones. Clearly you will have less control over the sound, but if the balance can be achieved simply by positioning these microphones strategically then it can work. As ever, don't be afraid of experimentation: scores of records before 1970 were recorded that way – and some of them were pretty damn funky.

Recording percussion is easier because players usually prefer to perform one instrument at a time. Percussion can be recorded with one microphone aimed very near the point of impact. Two microphones on two congas may help with the balance, but it isn't at all necessary. Just remember that percussion can have a wide dynamic range.

Getting the Levels Right

From the costliest of digital recording complexes to the cheapest cassette-based home "portastudios", the key to making successful recordings is in getting the levels right.

In the old days of analogue tape machines there were some golden rules of thumb:

RULE ONE: KEEP THE LEVELS BELOW +3 DB BUT HIGHER THAN –8 DB. Do whatever you have to do to achieve this level, including compression and manual fader riding.

RULE TWO: RECORD ONTO TAPE WITH A LITTLE EXTRA HIGH-END EQ. Then do the opposite on playback. This old chestnut was a way of keeping a true sound while removing some of that annoying background hiss.

RULE THREE: MAKE THE LEVELS A BIT HOTTER. In analogue, the disadvantages of a bit of "tape compression" (a natural result of too much level) were always accepted to be less than the disadvantages of tape noise.

After you've got the microphones set up, and the foldback sorted out, there remains only the sticky subject of levels. It's rather important, of course, to make sure that the signal being recorded is of an acceptable level – not too high, not too low – so that it sounds alright when it's replayed. Well, that's the theory, anyway.

This is all very well for old-fashioned analogue recording, but for digital audio it's a very different story. There are no golden rules now. It's true that very low levels will lower the digital specification of the recording, but it's nothing like as bad as tape noise. JUST MAKE SURE YOU DON'T GO WITH TOO HIGH LEVELS – DIGITAL DISTORTION MAKES AN AWFUL RACKET.

Tape: Reel-to Real-time

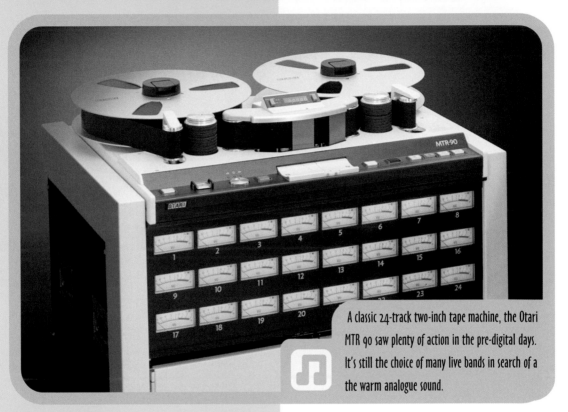

A classic 24-track two-inch tape machine, the Otari MTR 90 saw plenty of action in the pre-digital days. It's still the choice of many live bands in search of the warm analogue sound.

Even if you don't record using any kind of tape at all, you may nevertheless find that an understanding of the old method is helpful in less obvious ways. For this discussion, "tape" will refer to analogue, magnetic, reel-to-reel, brown, shiny-on-one-side, old-fashioned recording tape. All tape is fundamentally the same and all tape-machines share the same fundamentals. Home cassette tape is essentially the same as professional two-inch-tape – the big stuff is just wider, thicker and better-made.

When tape was first widely used for recording in the 1940s, it was a quarter of an inch wide tape and ran at 15 inches per second (IPS). It was noisy and

tended to break a lot, but it was far less expensive than making a "waxing" (a vinyl record) for every take. Above all, you could re-use it time and time again. Also – and this was the most exciting thing – it was editable. The whole concept of producing records as we know it flows directly from the advent of tape-editing. Herbert Von Karajan, the legendary conductor of the Berlin Philharmonic Orchestra, was one of the first to see its potential. While conducting and "producing" an orchestral recording he could be heard bemoaning the fact that the orchestra would always play the first movement best on Monday morning, the slow second movement best on Wednesday morning, and the fast final movement best on Friday afternoon. He realized that he could join these three days into one perfect hour simply by using a razor blade and some sticky tape. Thus, the magic of the record business was born.

Already by 1955, it was clear that no one would ever perform a record all the way through in one take. Even Elvis Presley's "perfect" vocals were cobbled together from many individual performances. And that was in the days of mono (one-track) tape recording. How was this magic done? The band first recorded the music without the vocals many times over until a "perfect" version was razor-bladed together. Then Elvis would sing over the tape of the music and both were recorded together onto another one-track tape recorder, thus making a "final mix" with every take. After a vocal recording session with Elvis, the producer would have perhaps 20 takes on tape - every one a "final mix'" version of the record. Next, the producer would painstakingly listen to all twenty versions and choose a chorus, verse, line or a word from each one where Elvis had sung it particularly

Luciano Berio was a music technology pioneer with his tape experiments of the 1950s.

Even Elvis used a version of the studio trickery we take for granted today. Many of his greatest early hits were composites constructed from different takes of the same song.

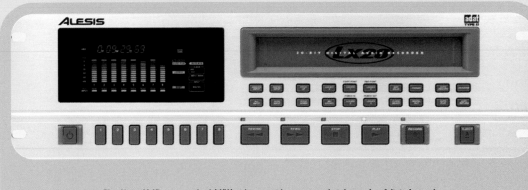

The Alesis ADAT uses standard S-VHS video cartridges to record eight tracks of digital sound.

well. Finally, he would razor-blade together all the best bits and copy the result to a new tape. It was a slow (but very effective) process. And Elvis probably never even knew about it.

When two- and four-track formats became available, overdubbing became the norm. This is when subsequent takes are recorded onto the same piece and at the same place on the tape (but alongside) as the takes recorded earlier. The trick here is that the machine is able to play back the previously recorded tracks while recording the new material at the same point on the tape, all the while keeping the tracks SYNCHRONIZED ("in-sync"). Cleverer still, the machine can listen to the already-recorded material on a given track and then suddenly "drop" into the record mode on the same track, only to "drop" out again moments later and resume playing back the earlier material. In this way, corrections and replacements could be done to a performance without the need for a razor blade. This requires a sophisticated tape machine "head", one which is able to play back and then record and then play back again with seamless, lightning accuracy. The system became known as selective synchronization, or "sel-sync". This remains at the heart of all formats of multi-track tape recording.

By 1973, tape machines were widely available in 16 and 24-track formats, recording on two-inch tape. These tapes ran either at 15 IPS (usually with the fashionable Dolby noise reduction system) or at 30 IPS which gave a better sound quality and needed no Dolby, but used expensive tape very quickly – running at 30 IPS, the longest tapes ran for just 30 minutes.

Even 24 tracks was not enough for the producers of the 1970s who began to use a device called a synchronizer which could make two 24-track machines run in mechanical tandem.

The first commercial digital recording machines appeared at the start of the 1980s. They used the modern digital system of analogue-to-digital converters and binary (computer) systems, but the storage medium was still traditional magnetic tape running on the same mechanical reel-to-reels at the same old 15 IPS.

The next development came in the arena of two-track MASTERING machines. Everyone realized that, regardless of how clean and wonderful the overdubbing was, it was the format of the final stereo master that mattered the most. By 1984, most professionals were still mastering (or "mixing down") onto the old analogue two-track machines. Things would soon change. That same year, the video cassette war was finally won by JVC's VHS format and Sony was stuck with the now unmarketable Betamax format. Yet soon every recording studio had a digital mastering device that stored the information on Betamax tapes. Known as the F1, it was the immediate precursor to the DAT format and worked in exactly the same way, using the same quality and specifications. No one really understood why every record was passing through a Betamax player before being released, but it seemed to be the done thing.

By 1988, Betamax had been usurped by the little king called DAT. Tiny, convenient, reliable, stylish, easily storable, DAT is still the choice of many professionals and there is nothing yet on the horizon to displace it as the most reliable mastering format.

Eight-track DAT tape machines – A-DAT or HI-8 – appeared in the early 1990s and soon became a staple of the industry. Cheap, reliable and convenient, these tiny and easy-to-use multitracks were used for home studios, location recordings and (when linked together to provide 24 or more tracks) in top studios. Only with the near-perfection of Digital audio in 1999 did the ADAT frenzy finally begin to wane.

Multi-track tape did not have such a gradual demise. The plateau of 48-track analogue tape and digital tape machines remained until the mid-1990s when the world suddenly went computer mad. Very few records are now made with tape. The world of digital audio and direct-to-disk recording is faster, cheaper, cleaner, easier to manipulate, in fact, it's more EVERYTHING. Tape is dead.

The Alesis CADI is one system for linking together a large number of ADAT machines and controlling them from a central unit.

Although the popularity of the ADAT has been usurped by the growth of hard-disk recording systems it remains the format of choice in many small studios across the world.

Neat, compact and self-contained, this is the face of recording in the 21st century. And not a spool of tape in sight.

CHAPTER 8

THE RECORD STUDIO IN YOUR COMPUT

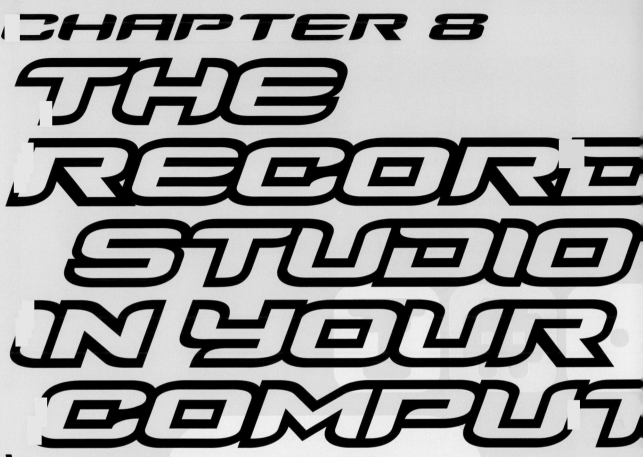

A computer is simply a device for processing binary data very quickly. A computer circuit is either "off" (0) or "on" (1). This is the lowest level that all programs – word processors, spreadsheets, games, digital audio/MIDI – must eventually address. You see, it's basically all just a load of old ones and zeros.

ProTools is the software of choice for most top-end industry professionals.

All computers have an OPERATING SYSTEM, which provides a user interface to enable PROGRAMS (or APPLICATIONS) to run on the computer. Some companies (such as Microsoft) specialize in producing only software, whilst others (such as Apple Computers) produce both the hardware and software integrated into a complete package. By far the most popular operating system in use on PCs is Microsoft Windows, although it is not necessarily the best OS for running digital audio.

Using Computers

At first glance it would seem that the computer is the perfect tool for processing digital audio. After sound has been converted into digital "bits" by an ADC (*see page 34*) it becomes a stream of zeros and ones, which are the "meat and potatoes" for a computer. However, the computational power and speed required to process the information contained in just one second of 16-bit audio is phenomenal and puts a great strain on all the components of a PC, from the CPU to the hard disk drive. Indeed, most professional Digital Audio Workstations (DAWs) rely on custom-built add-on DSP cards to take most of the strain off the CPU, ensure smooth operation and provide the maximum number of audio record and playback tracks.

Unlike samplers that record sound directly into internal RAM, the DAW records and plays back directly to the hard disk drive (HDD). This places a very heavy load on hard disk, which usually has a fairly easy time with programs such as word processors or MIDI sequencers – all it really has to do is launch programs, load previously saved information into RAM, or save work. Some graphically intensive games and streaming video applications can put a heavy load on the hard disk, which can result in jittery graphics, but may become totally unusable with audio that necessarily demands very precise timing.

Digital Audio Workstations (DAWs) come in three flavours:

1. Purpose-built Systems

This type of Digital Audio Workstation is designed from the bottom up, uses its own hardware, operating systems and file formats. Purpose-built systems are invariably the most expensive. Examples are the Fairlight MF3 and the AMS Audioframe.

2. Host Computer With DSP Card

This is the most popular type of system in professional use. It consists of a PC with an Intel Pentium processor running Microsoft Windows OS (sometimes called a "Wintel Box") or an Apple Power Macintosh running the Mac OS. Each system has added PCI cards and audio interfaces. This is the best-selling type of system, with many MIDI/audio software companies providing direct or indirect support for third party hardware. Some examples are Digidesign ProTools, Soundscape and Sonic Solutions.

3. Host-based Systems

This is the most recent development, made possible only by today's high-speed processor chips. On

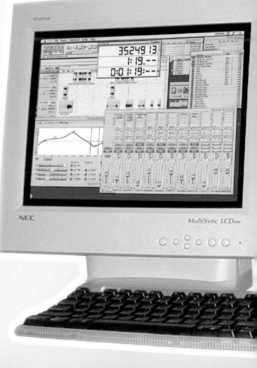

such systems, all the processing is performed by the host computer with no extra DSP hardware being required (although some kind of audio interface with ADCs and DACs is required to get the audio into and out of the computer). Two examples are Sonic Foundry's Vegas and Nuendo by Steinberg.

How To Buy

So what are the requirements for a modern computer-based audio recording system?

- A Macintosh or Wintel Box.
- A hard disk drive, in ADDITION to your computer's main HDD, or AT LEAST with a separate PARTITION.
- An audio interface.
- Suitable Software.

RULE NUMBER ONE FOR SMART DIGITAL AUDIO SHOPPERS: as all of the above components are likely to come from different manufacturers, the best policy is to buy the WHOLE system from one reputable dealer. The advantages are manifold. To begin with, you'll get the pre-configured system working from the start – this easily the hardest and most frustrating part of the process. You'll also get a better deal that will work out much cheaper than buying separate components from different sources. Finally, YOU ONLY HAVE ONE PERSON TO BLAME IF IT DOESN'T WORK PROPERLY. There is nothing worse than buying different parts from different sources only to be told when something goes wrong (and it invariably WILL) by one supplier that it's the fault of a component you bought from a different supplier (which they invariably WILL).

Final Words

If you already own a computer, you should seriously consider keeping that for whatever purpose it currently serves. Buy a new system SOLELY for MIDI/audio use.

If you're on a tight budget, invest in one of the cheaper "cut down" versions of Cubase or Logic and run it on your PC with a only few audio tracks and features. This enables you to test the water and upgrade when funds are available. If you choose this route, back up all your existing work and reformat your hard disk drive into two partitions. Use one partition for your system and programs and the second partition purely for audio. If you use a Macintosh, use Extensions Manager to make a separate set of extensions for your audio system.

Audio Cards

To get audio in and out of your computer, you will need some kind of audio/sound card. Modern Apple Macintoshes have a built-in 16-bit, 44.1k stereo sound card which is usable (if a little on the noisy side for professional applications). There is a bewildering choice of audio/sound cards available. Most are designed to work with both Mac and PC, fitting into a standard PCI slot. All you need is an appropriate "driver", which comes with the card.

Your choice of audio card will be governed by several factors:

1. How does it sound?

This may seem obvious, but no amount of studying technical specifications can take the place of listening to the card in operation with a decent monitoring system. You should be able to get a comprehensive demonstration of any system that you're considering buying in any decent music store (if you can't, then you should take your cash elsewhere), although auditioning a friend's set-up is invariably more useful. In practice, any system on sale should sound pretty good – especially if you are used to hearing analogue systems.

2. How much does it cost?

There are so many PCI audio cards available that bargains are always available. You may be able to find something for half the price that it sold for six months earlier. Buying a MIDI/audio sequencer bundled with an audio card can also save you money. You should beware of buying second hand. Most people who are selling computer equipment have an unrealistic idea of its value, and you have little comeback if things go wrong.

3. Don't pay for features that you don't need.

What are you going to use your set-up for? Do you already have (or intend to get) gear that needs a special interface? If you already have an Alesis ADAT or other equipment that uses a "lightpipe" optical interface, then buying a card which includes such an interface would be a sensible idea. If you are an analogue junkie, then a card with a large number of analogue "ins" and "outs" would be a good idea. Many and various digital inputs and outputs are relatively easy (and cheap) to implement on an audio card, but multiple analogue connections can be quite tricky. These will require multiple DACs, which will be housed in a separate external unit ("breakout box").

Digital Jargon to Keep You Awake at Night

Any audio card worth its salt should offer "full duplex" operation. This simply refers to the ability to record and playback audio at the same time. This should be the norm on most modern systems, but you should check this out if you're buying a cheap audio card for a Wintel box.

LATENCY (a figure measured in milliseconds) refers to the amount of time taken for the audio that you're recording to be heard through the output. This isn't a problem if you have an external mixing desk to monitor what's being recorded together with the audio playback from your computer, but if you are monitoring directly from the card it can cause timing problems while you are recording.

The wild and wonderful Waldorf Wave plug-in synthesizer – even virtual instruments can't resist using exposed "wires".

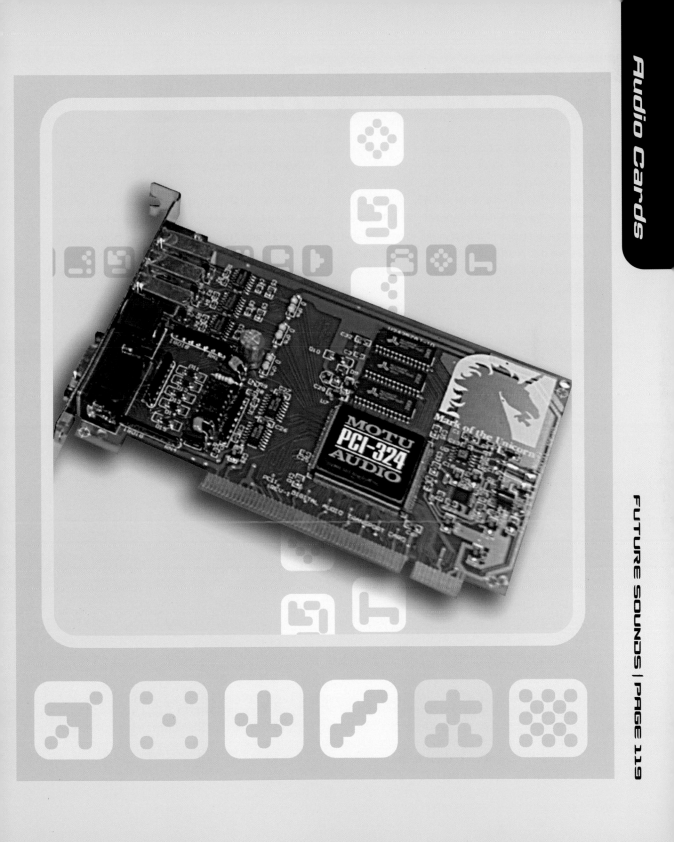

Digital Versus Analogue

In an analogue system, information is conveyed by varying a continuous parameter, such as a voltage on a wire or the magnetic flux strength on a piece of recording tape. When an analogue signal is converted back into sound by a loudspeaker, it contains the sum of all degradations introduced at the various stages through which it has passed. This sets a limit to the number of stages an analogue signal can be passed before it becomes unusable. Nevertheless,

some of these degradations – such as the SATURATION effect produced when recording high-level signals to analogue tape, or the HARMONIC DISTORTION produced when valve guitar amps are overdriven – can be pleasing to the ear. Indeed, they have played an important part in the way the sound of music has evolved.

An ideal digital system has the same characteristics as an ideal analogue system: both should be totally transparent and reproduce the

Digital technology allows greater flexibility for treating signals than its analogue counterpart.

original sound without error. Unfortunately, such conditions are rare. In truth, analogue and digital equipment both fall short of the ideal. It's just that digital gear falls short by a smaller degree. The sound quality of a well-engineered digital system is independent of the recording medium, depending solely on the quality of the conversion process (both DAC and ADC). Digital processing also offers tremendous opportunities denied to analogue signals. Because digital audio employs the binary language spoken by computers, manipulation and processing can take place within this relatively cheap, mass-produced medium.

Mark Of The Unicorn (MOTU) produces a wide range of digital audio gear designed to work with Macintosh or PC platforms.

More Technical Stuff

After the quality of the ADC, the most critical criterion of the process is CLOCKING. For digital audio to retain its sonic integrity, the individual samples it uses must arrive at the output at exactly the right time. This is made possible by locking them to an extremely accurate digital clock (known as WORD CLOCK), so that they are perfectly synchronized. If the samples are not perfectly synched, unwanted artifacts – such as clicking, stuttering and popping noises – start to appear. The degree with which a digital clock deviates from perfect time is called JITTER. A low-jitter clock will make the audio signal sound better, and is, therefore, most important for digital system performance. Most problems that occur within a digital audio system comes from using unstable clock sources.

As we saw in Chapter 3, the two main factors relating to an ADC are the sampling rate and bit resolution. Standard audio CDs use a sampling rate of 44.1 kHz at 16 bits. This means that the analogue input to the ADC is sampled 44,100 times per second using a 16-bit digital word length. This is because 44,100 Hz is slightly more than double the highest frequency that we are capable of hearing (20 kHz), and 16 bits provide a dynamic range (16 x 6 = 96 dB) which is considered adequate to accommodate sounds from the quietest whisper to the loudest transient. But what actually happens when this raw binary data is processed by a computer or other digital device?

By its very nature, sampling involves the expression of some infinitely variable quantity by discreet or stepped values. This is known as QUANTIZING, and can be considered as similar to the quantization function in MIDI sequencers. In an attempt to keep the technical stuff to a minimum, let's just say that quantizing is not perfect. Indeed, it will always introduce errors or some description. At high signal levels, quantizing error effectively becomes noise. As the audio level falls, the quantizing error of an ideal ADC becomes more strongly correlated with the signal. This results in distortion. As we have seen (and you have probably heard), analogue distortion can be very pleasing to the ear. Digital distortion, on the other hand, is particularly nasty.

If the quantizing error can be decorrelated from the input in some way, the system can remain linear but noisy. A function called DITHER performs this task by making the action of the quantizer (ADC) unpredictable, giving the system a noise floor like an analogue system. Dither is also important when converting data to a lower bit-depth. The digital words need to be shortened in some way. If you have been working with a 24-bit digital word length and you want to convert to 16 bits for CD production, what happens to the extra 8 bits? Without dither, these extra 8 bits are simply thrown away, leading to a compromizing of the audio quality. When dither is applied, the low-level information in these extra 8 bits is retained, giving higher quality audio to the final 16-bit CD. This may be pretty esoteric stuff but it is important in maintaining the best audio integrity in your music.

One man and his tools – a digital recording studio for the 21st century.

CHAPTER 9
SETTING YOUR OWN STUDIO

Most of you will probably want to create and record your own music and be able to carry the process through to a finished product on CD. This is perfectly possible at relatively little cost.

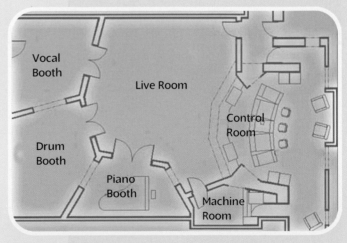

Vocal Booth

Live Room

Control Room

Drum Booth

Piano Booth

Machine Room

In this chapter we'll take a look at some of the issues relating to the idea of setting a small domestic recording studio.

Big desk? Small desk? Virtual desk? These are among the critical decisions you'll need to make.

Begin by asking yourself this question: What do you want to use your studio for? If you want to produce music that relies solely on pre-sampled and synthesized sound sources, then you will only need a computer (the more powerful the better), some software and a CD burner. The samplers and synths can be software based and your music can remain in the digital domain until you play back the final CD (to the amazement of your friends and family).

This "solo" approach can be very creative and rewarding. After a time, however, you'll probably find that you could use some outside input. You may want to use a singer or some acoustic musicians. Some instruments are extremely difficult to emulate using samples, largely because they are so tonally varied – the human voice is an obvious example – so some other means of naturally incorporating these sounds into your music is needed. To do this you must add a decent microphone and microphone pre-amp to your system. Money carefully spent in this area is never wasted because no amount of computer wizardry can improve a poorly recorded signal. When recording sounds using a microphone you will obviously need to keep out extraneous sounds that you don't want to get onto your recording. This brings us neatly on to the tricky subject of sound proofing and acoustic treatments.

Traditionally, the most costly aspect of setting up a recording studio has been in designing and building spaces that will keep the sound you're making in, and all others out. But, unless you intend to record a full band playing together live, you can avoid most of this expense.

working Environment

Your studio should be designed as user-friendly and comfortable. If you're going to be working mainly on your own, make sure the gear that you most often need to get your hands is easily accessible from your "producer's chair". A comfortable, armless office chair is ideal for this function, especially if has wheels so that you can easily "skate" over to tweak a piece of kit which is just out of reach.

Your mix position should typically be in the centre of the "sweet-spot" between your monitor speakers. This is the position where you and the two speakers form a perfect triangle. Your computer screen, keyboard, mixing desk and MIDI master keyboard should be directly in front of you. This can be a little tricky to achieve in practice, but time spent in the planning stage is rarely wasted. You can buy (or build) a tabletop to hold the equipment listed above. It's also useful to have a pull-out drawer beneath the table to hold your MIDI master keyboard. This can then be pushed underneath when it's not required.

You'll be spending plenty of time in your studio so try to make your working environment as comfortable as possible.

The positioning of your computer is another matter. Computers are noisy beasts. They use fans to cool their internal components: drives and CD-ROMs also generate a lot of noise. This may not be apparent at first, but you will later find that it becomes an annoying cacophony when you're trying to work. The best solution is to put your computer either outside the room or box it in with some acoustically absorbent material. If you take this approach, take care to avoid obstructing the cooling vents or blocking the air circulation around it.

Other sources of noise may be more difficult to deal with. Household appliances such as fridges, washing machines and central heating systems not only throw out an alarming amount of mechanical noise but may also send all manner of clicks and spikes into your electrical mains supply. In such cases a MAINS POWER CONDITIONER may be needed to sort out the problem.

When it comes to recording vocals and "miked-up" instruments, you must be able to exclude unwanted sounds. Aircraft, sirens and motorcycles can be very intrusive and – if your studio is poorly sound-proofed – you may well end up being forced to re-record some sounds unless you can "gate-out" offending noises. Louder sound sources, such as close-miked guitar amps and saxophones, can easily drown-out background noise, and so should be less of a problem.

Your biggest challenge will be recording vocals. If pressed for time or money, it's worth experimenting by using other areas of your home – the kitchen, bathroom or a closet – or by lining a large cardboard box with foam, putting a microphone inside, and getting the singer to put it over his head to record the vocal. (Don't laugh,

there is certainly at least one top-selling album that was recorded in this way.) If you're doing the microphone recording in your control room, one old trick is to set up a stereo pair of microphones wired OUT OF PHASE with a "phase-reversal adapter") and perform into only one of them – in theory, any unwanted sound will enter both microphones and be cancelled out.

Monitoring Systems

Your own hi-fi system may be the best choice on which to monitor your recordings. Since it is the set-up on which you listen to most of your CDs it will give you a direct comparison to your own efforts. For the last 20 years or so, over 90% of chart music has been mixed on speakers designed for home use (predominantly Yamaha NS10s). If possible, it's a good idea to have one or two alternative sets of speakers – indeed, it's always useful to hear your music played back on as many different systems as possible.

Every studio needs at least one set of monitor speakers.

Audio and Midi

If you already work mostly with MIDI, using hardware samplers and synthesizers, you'll probably prefer to use combined MIDI/audio sequencing software, which concentrates on powerful MIDI facilities with audio incorporated. The "Big Four" in this area are E-Magic's Logic, Steinberg's Cubase VST/Cubasis, MOTU's Digital Performer, and Vision by Opcode. Conversely, if you want to work mainly with audio and add a limited degree of MIDI functionality, ProTools by Digidesign, Nuendo by Steinberg or Sonic Foundry's Vegas or Sound Forge software may be the answer.

People sometimes complain that there is no cut-down, MIDI-only version of the current popular software, and so are driven to use an older version. The old Atari ST still has its champions who favour its simplicity of use and solid timing. If you fall into this camp (or intend to work with MIDI only) this option provides a very cost-effective solution. Don't forget, though, if you intend to use MIDI-only software, an external mixer will be required to handle your MIDI devices.

It's more likely, however, that you'll want to take advantage of the current generation of cheap and powerful computers now available by opting for a combined MIDI/audio solution. This has the advantage of allowing you to record your MIDI instruments back into the computer as audio tracks and then mix the whole song from inside the computer. This option will give you the most control over your music, and, if you use an external digital desk, you can use this to control your sequencer via MIDI.

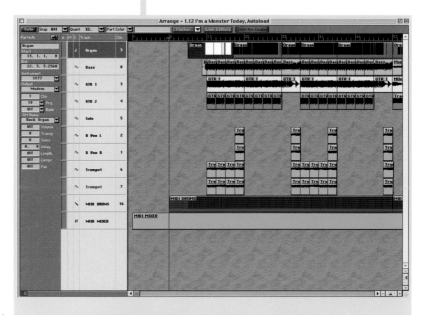

Most users opt for a MIDI/audio solution when choosing sequencing software.

Time spent planning your studio set-up and talking to other musicians, producers, engineers, and dealers is well spent. Although you will get conflicting opinions, some sort of pattern should soon emerge to help you make your choice.

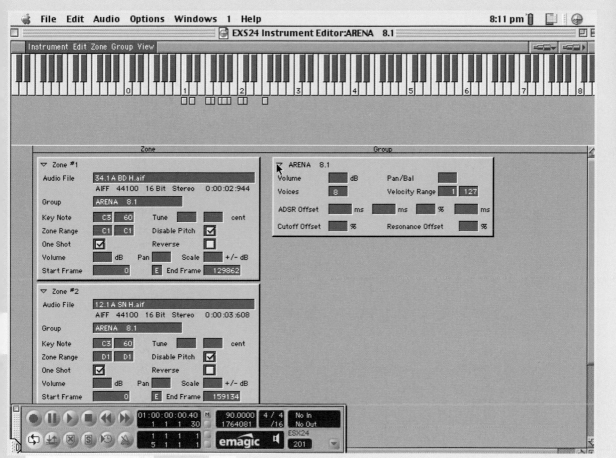

This virtual sampler is a generation beyond the old Akai workhorse and avoids problems of MIDI timing and a lack of desk channels.

Saving Yourself Cash

If money were no object, we would all buy ourselves top-flight SSL and Neve desks, Studer 24-track 2-inch analogue recorders, and state-of-the-art- everything else. Unfortunately, most of us can't afford anything like the hundreds and thousands of pounds that level of gear would cost. But that doesn't matter because now, for the first time, we can achieve results that are just as good, for far less money.

None of us likes to spend our hard-earned cash if we don't have to. A serious area of concern in putting together a recording studio is to identify areas where you can save money and those where skimping on cost would be counter-productive. The main thing to remember is that your recording chain is only as strong as its weakest link. It's just like buying a hi-fi system – spending heavily on one component to the detriment of others will not only fail to improve the sound but can show up the deficiencies in other gear.

Let's first consider the centrepiece of the studio – the computer. In Chapter 8 we discussed the merits of different computer platforms and their software and hardware. Our advice here is worth reiterating: IT IS COMPLETE FOLLY TO TRY AND SAVE MONEY BY BUYING A CHEAP PC FROM A LARGE-VOLUME, HEAVILY ADVERTISED BOX-SHIFTING STORE. These companies haven't a clue about the special requirements of running high-quality audio on a computer. Unless you're very computer-literate and know the Windows operating system inside out (and are capable of building your own PC from scratch), GO FOR AN APPLE MACINTOSH.

The computer is going to be at the very heart of your studio, so beware of false-economic cost-cutting in this area. As we've said before, buy your computer, drives, audio card and software package from a single reputable dealer. That way you'll get it all pre-configured and tested, with a technical back-up service and no chance of buck-passing when things go wrong. If this central component of your studio works properly, you should be able to add extra outboard stuff with few problems. If not, no amount of extraneous tackle will improve it. Also, the more gear that you buy from one single source, the more chance you have of getting a good deal, so get quotes from several of them, go along for demos, talk to them about your needs and see what they have to offer.

The Audio Card

The most important stage in getting audio into your computer is the analogue-to-digital converter. Money spent on a good quality ADC is never wasted. Huge numbers of PCI audio cards are available for personal computers, so here are a number of criteria that should inform your choice:

1. Does your software support the audio card?
In order to communicate with a PCI audio card, the software will have to make use of a DRIVER. Drivers are required for your computer to work with add-on hardware, such as disk drives, printers and PCI cards. Some audio cards are directly supported from within the software. Usually, hardware which is manufactured by the software company will interface most comfortably – E-Magic's Logic software and Audiowerk PCI card is a good example. Generally speaking, most popular software will also support other manufacturers' cards. There are also a number of other driver protocols, the

most comprehensive being ASIO. This is used by several software manufacturers, most notably Steinberg, who don't make any PCI hardware of their own.

2. Does the audio card give you the number of inputs and outputs that you require?

If you already have a digital recorder or mixer, you'll probably want a card that has digital input and output connections. If you're using an analogue desk, you'll need a card with the maximum number of analogue outputs so that you can mix directly from of the computer. Bear in mind that the performance of the Digital Audio Converters (DACs) is just as important as that of ADCs. And the word here is that *real* quality doesn't come cheap. Check

The two faces of digital music: recordings may be tape-based (left) or made using a computer (right).

out reviews in reputable music technology magazines and always be prepared to listen to recommendations from other users. The highest-quality PCI cards offering analogue inputs and outputs will have the converters located in a BREAKOUT BOX connected externally to the computer. Since these important components are housed outside the computer they are consequently much less susceptible to noise interference.

3. How much will it all cost?

For many of us this will come at the very top of the list. There are, however, always bargains to be had, especially if you are prepared to be working around six months behind the cutting edge of technology. For instance, the Korg 12/12 PCI card cost around £700 on its release during 1998. It can now be had for less than £200. It's a buyers market, so you'll do well to haggle.

4. What facilities do I really need?

Lots of manufacturers are offering 24-bit, 96 kHz audio cards. Bear in mind that your final format will be a 16-bit, 44.1 kHz audio CD. As we've seen in previous chapters, a higher bit depth will give a wider bandwidth and so is useful to work with until you finally "dither" down to 16-bit when you master. A 96 kHz sampling rate, however, is less important. You'll need twice the processing and twice the hard disk space to store your 96 kHz audio and the final result will probably not benefit from such effort and expense.

5 What do the professionals use?

When it comes to the crunch, the professionals tend to use Digidesign TDM hardware and either ProTools, Logic or Digital Performer software. People working in the music business are, of necessity, conservative in their choice of gear. After all, they spend a great deal of time developing skills and their own ways of working. Any piece of kit that enhances this is wholeheartedly embraced. Professionals will tolerate a temperamental piece of equipment so long as it works wonderfully most of the time. But when it comes to the central process of recording and editing, the gear's performance must be beyond reproach.

The best recommendation for any piece of equipment is word of mouth. If someone brings in some new technology to a recording session and everyone is impressed by its performance, then this positive reaction will spread. Manufacturers are well aware that this is the best way of promoting a new piece of equipment and often hold demonstrations in major studios and leave gear there for assessment. But the converse is also true. If a product is found to be sorely lacking in sound quality, ease-of-use, reliability and inter-connectivity, it will be summarily dismissed. Such negative first impressions can be very difficult to reverse later, as some have learned to their cost.

6. What's the bottom line?

There are no easy answers, but here are two important considerations:

- **GO FOR THE MOST POWERFUL COMPUTER YOU CAN AFFORD**. Computer technology is mass-produced and will therefore give you the most "bang-for-the-buck" in raw processing power. Get an Apple Macintosh or a Wintel box from a dealer specializing in computer audio.

- **IF YOU ARE NEW TO COMPUTERS GET AN APPLE MACINTOSH.** If you are PC-literate, you probably already own a PC. In this case, get a cheap, cut down version of a well-known MIDI/audio sequencer (there are occasionally free versions available – check it out on the Internet) and install it on the PC you already own. Almost all software manufacturers will specify a bare minimum of a Pentium processor for their PC based products, although this is usually because they haven't tested it with older processors. Try it out: you never know, it may work fine.

MOTU digital systems combine PCI card with an outboard "Breakout Box" to connect the computer to a conventional mixing desk.

If you're particularly wealthy you might just be able to run to a computerized desk with automated faders.

Getting It Right:
What to Buy and What to Avoid

Putting together the perfect studio is all about balance. It's about getting enough gear for not too much money; enough comfort for not too much money; enough quality for not too much money; enough choice for not too much money. Obviously, you want to get it right.

Desks

This is the tricky one. A desk could easily be the most expensive purchase you ever make for your music. It's the heart of the studio and it will be the single most important factor in determining the quality of your sound. You need to start with some

Rebirth may be the best video game ever — it's also a pretty neat virtual drum and bass box.

basic decisions. The debate between "real" and "virtual" desks will go on forever. It's not about technology or about "the latest thing", it's more likely to be about style. Some people deeply love computers and prefer to have everything in one box. Computer-screen desks are now widely available and they represent no compromize in quality or options. You may get more features for your money. Of course, the computer has only the workings of the desk inside it and you will have to also buy the connection box for all your gear to hook up to it. This box converts any plugged-in source (microphones, guitars and keyboards) into a digital signal for the computer to manipulate. The quality of this conversion (the ADC) will vary widely according to the price of the model. While the virtual desk itself is relatively cheap, bear in mind the cost of the ADC and connections box as part of the whole package. Think about what level of quality you require (the cheapest ones often sound pretty rough. Think about how many inputs you are likely to need at any one time: Eight? Twelve? Sixteen? More?

A mixing desk could be the single most costly element of your studio.

Traditional desks have a lot going for them. For some, the fact that have one knob for each control, instead of a mouse covering all of them, can be crucial. In the heat of a session or a mix, it's helpful to be able to instantly reach over for a control without even looking at it. Furthermore, real desks don't ever "crash".

The available range of desks is endless. Again, think about the overall quality of sound and how many inputs will you need at one time. With real desks, you need to consider every input needed, including those needed for tape machines and digital audio channels: virtual desks need only be connected to the external sound sources since the digital links are already built-in; "real" desks require an actual lead for every source and every track. Furthermore, hardware desks need a separate channel for each effect used – virtual desks are kitted out with built-in plug-in effects.

Hardware desks can be very reasonably priced. A good quality 8-channel desk can be bought for less than £500. Even excellent-quality 32-channel desks (such as the world-beating Mackie console) can be bought for as little as £3000. It's also worth looking at second-hand desks: as more and more people go for the virtual options the market is flooded with good deals.

Leads

If you treat this subject too lightly it will ALWAYS comes back to haunt you. Few people realize the number of leads they will require or how much they cost to buy. Fewer still consider that the positioning of gear can greatly affect the budget required for leads. If your mixing desk is ten feet away from your keyboard rack, it will be twice as expensive to connect as it would at a distance of five feet. It's a good idea to plan your set-up using string and a measuring tape to figure out the possible distances and costs. If you find a good deal on an 8-track ADAT recorder you will need sixteen leads (eight

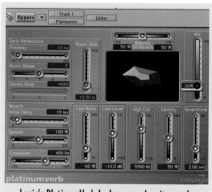

Logic's PlatinumVerb looks as good as it sounds.

inputs and eight outputs) however far it is to the desk. Every keyboard or synth module requires at least one lead – some may need up to ten. You may need only one or two microphone cables but these are the most expensive. And don't forget about MAINS and MIDI leads.

The Audio Recorder

This decision is usually a relatively easy one. You may decide to begin with nothing but a sequencer. Equally, you may decide to start with a cheap or used ADAT recorder or use an old analogue machine. But for a growing number of people there is no realistic alternative to using computer-based digital audio. The major programs, such as LOGIC and CUBASE, already have the software to allow you to

record audio on your computer. As you've already seen in Chapter 8, all you need is a sound card.

If possible, try to get hold of a regular stereo DAT machine of some sort. They are easily the most commonly used format for mixdowns, and are also handy for making back-ups. And if you intend to turn your recordings into a commercial releases, a stereo DAT master is the best way of getting your work of art to the manufacturer.

Effects

The buzz of the moment is definitely for "plug-in" effects. New virtual versions of old effects are seemingly released every day. They're always cheaper than their hardware equivalents and many are available as Freeware or Shareware on the Web. The modern home recordist can build up a brilliant studio that contains no real effects boxes at all. Others prefer the "real" thing – effects boxes are continually becoming cheaper than ever. In audio terms, few can tell the difference between the two.

Drum Machines

Many people continue to use drum machines despite having a full computer sequencer set-up. Some clearly prefer banging forcefully on the buttons of a dedicated drum box than tapping keys on a computer keyboard. Others claim the

Roland's legendary TB-303 single-handedly fuelled the Acid House movement.

sounds straight out of the drum box have a "punch" that samplers can't provide. But whatever the reason, it's perfectly valid and it's very easy and reliable to run.

The king and queen of all drum machines are the legendary Roland TR909 and the TR808 models. Literally thousands of hit records have used these drum sounds – even if the sounds have been sampled rather than coming from the Real McCoy. If you choose not to buy either of these machines (they are long out of production and can fetch high second-hand prices) you may want to keep a disk of their sampled sounds handy.

Ancient drum machines without MIDI are probably best avoided.

Keyboards

Keyboards (including synthesizers and other sound modules) come in many shapes, flavours, colours and sizes. Somewhere out there is your "perfect" keyboard. The main dividing line is between digital/sample-based models and those which use traditional analogue principles.

Many of the analogue classics are still in heavy use. These includes such venerable names as the MiniMoog, MemoryMoog, Roland Juno 106, OSCAR, EDP Wasp, Sequential Circuits Prophet 5, ARP 2600, Roland SH-101, and any of the older Korgs, to name but a few. They are known for the warmth, "fatness" and purity of their sounds. The Juno 106 and the MiniMoog are still frequently used for their powerful bass sounds.

Somewhere in between old analogue classics and the modern-day "whiz kids" are the original digital synths. These keyboards were thought to be magical when they first appeared in the late 1970s: the sounds of the PPG WAVE, Sequential Circuits Prophet VS and the Korg DW series are all once again very fashionable.

The next generation of digital synths were known for their versatility and clarity. The first classic of this area was the Yamaha DX-7, which was largely

For REALLY fat bass lines you can't do much better than a Roland Juno-106.

The Boss Dr Rhythm provides powerful drum sounds.

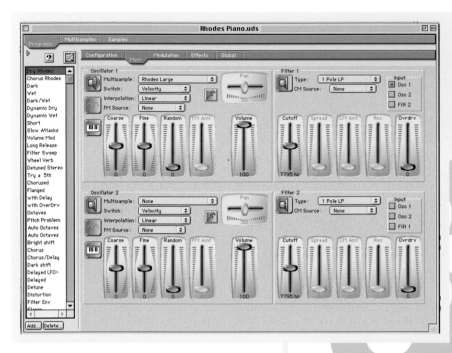

The BitHeadz Unity virtual sampler offers all the standard features of a hardware digital sampler.

responsible for the most of the sounds Of The 1980s. The Korg M1 remains the best-selling keyboard of all time, mostly because of its sample-style sounds. The M1 has a passable preset version of just about every "real" instrument from piano to flute. Other modern "digital" classics include the Roland JD-800, the Korg Wavestation, the Kurzweil K-2000, and the Oberheim Matrix series. These are the sounds of the 1990s.

Digital Samplers

Dedicated samplers deserve a mention of their own because just about everybody one engaged in modern music-making needs one. Without a shadow of a doubt, the king of samplers is the AKAI S-3000. There have been many AKAI models since the first S900 (mono) and S1000 (stereo) classics. The S3000 continued in this tradition. If you decide to buy a used AKAI sampler, make sure that the blue light in the LCD screen is as bright as possible. If it's too dull it may have seen a bit too much action. There are, of course, excellent alternatives. Models

produced by Roland, Yamaha and EMU all have a dedicated following. For many people, though, the technical differences are not so important as the price. There is a growing trend towards the use of software samplers (or "virtual samplers"). These may be worth considering since they have many potential advantages:

1. They are already inside the computer and require no desk channels or leads.

2. They can be loaded up with a set of sounds with just a click of the mouse.

3. They present no MIDI timing problems and need no MIDI leads or additional boxes.

4. They can cost considerably less than then a real box.

As ever, the choice is yours.

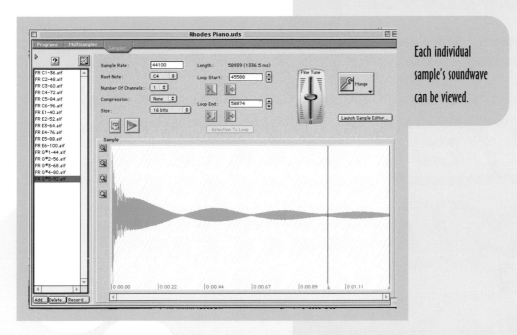

Each individual sample's soundwave can be viewed.

Sample keygroups are arranged across a virtual keyboard on the screen.

CHAPTER 10
SELLING YOUR MUSIC
The Traditional Route

Grandmaster Flash —
pioneers on the radical
rap revolution.

Perhaps the only remaining truth from the Sixties is that old adage "Rock 'n' Roll will never die". Sadly, this ongoing afterlife presents the biggest problem facing contemporary pop musicians. So long as record companies have a back catalogue to package and repackage again and again, "new" music will always have an enemy. The first time we saw this phenomenon was with the introduction of the compact disc during the 1980s, when both equipment manufacturers and record companies managed to sell us what we already owned in a slightly different form. The hi-fi people sold us new CD players and whole new stereo systems involving smaller boxes with more LED lights and remote controls. And the record companies managed to sell us huge amounts of music from the previous two decades on CD. Not long after that, we were offered the same music again, this time "digitally remastered". Few people inside or outside the industry really understand what this meant, but that didn't stop the Top 40 filling up with old music. This problem was hardly aided by the advertising industry – jeans companies alone have put nearly three dozen Golden Oldies back in the charts over the past two decades.

All of this is teaches us one simple lesson. Record companies, like all businesses, are interested in only one thing: maximizing profits by making the smallest possible investment. While this may seem obvious, this fact is often conveniently overlooked. It is true that there will always be some companies that wish to be involved in certain kinds of music because (apparently) they simply like, respect and enjoy the music, but no company can survive for long without also respecting the bottom line. Indeed, few artists can remain with a company for long if they do not respect the company's respect for the bottom line.

This is not to say that artists should become businessmen, or that they ought to perform with dollar bills in mind, but rather that they should be aware of what the record companies have utmost in their minds at all times.

The Business

A record deal is like a bargain in a street market. There are no rules. The number on the price tag is only a rough guide to the opening bid, and sometimes there may be no price tag at all. The buyer (the record company) pays only what he thinks he can get away with and the seller (the artist) receives only what he can get. Record deals range from the sublime, where the artist has enough cards to demand large advances and huge slices of the profits, to the ridiculous, where the artist has virtually no cards and must settle for no advance and a slim hope of a very small slice of a profit (which may not even legally exist). Strangely, however, it occasionally turns out that the "sublime" deal bears no fruit, while the "ridiculous" deal makes an artist very happy and very rich. Just like a street market, you see?

So how do you figure out whether the deal you are being offered is a good one? Start with this golden rule: DON'T BOTHER TRYING TO BE A LAWYER. This book does not purport to teach you about law. As a musician or pop star you will probably not benefit from a detailed knowledge of

Home studios take it straight from the bedroom to the board room.

music law. Indeed, it's highly unlikely that most musicians would ever have the time or inclination to learn more than "enough to be dangerous" – all that time and energy should really be spent on the music.

There is a tendency among musicians to be "legally paranoid". The most creative and sensitive souls seem also to be the most worried. Perhaps the excitement generated by making their own music naturally leads to an over-protective feeling. Perhaps the ego-massage of hearing their own music being produced clouds their thinking. Whatever the reason, too many musicians jump too quickly to unjustified and self-defeating conclusions.

Many feel a need to take premature legal advice. Few are aware of the acceptability of a "non-legal" professional relationship. While this may not always be the right option, it's a good idea to think carefully about the need for a lawyer before instinctively making what may prove to be an expensive phone call.

Management Deals

This idea generally holds for all management deals: keep it informal. You may be surprised to learn that many of history's most successful artist-manager relationships have been entirely oral. In the early days of an artist's career there is little to be gained from a written agreement. It all comes down to trust, and if that does not already exist then the relationship is probably on a tenuous footing from the start. Certainly there are situations where such formal agreements will work. If you were offered a management deal at an early stage in your career on by someone with a well-known track record in your area of the market, then such an agreement might well be a risk worth taking. But the majority of successful management relationships start out as trusting, mutually respecting friendships that require no contracts to be signed. Worry about that sort of thing when things start to hot up and the figures on offer begin to resemble telephone numbers.

So do you need a written contract or not? The important point is to ask yourself why a contract is necessary. Who does it benefit and how? If you feel that the balance is too one-sided (or if you just have an instinctive bad feeling) then put off making a decision for a week and find someone with whom you can discuss your concerns.

Getting Ripped Off

For many musicians, the greatest fear is the idea of having their work "stolen". More often than not, such concerns are a waste of time and opportunity. It's extremely unlikely that anyone would have the wherewithal to reproduce and sell your songs before you do. If your music is good enough to "steal", then it's also probably good enough to get you a deal in the first place. It is also unlikely that

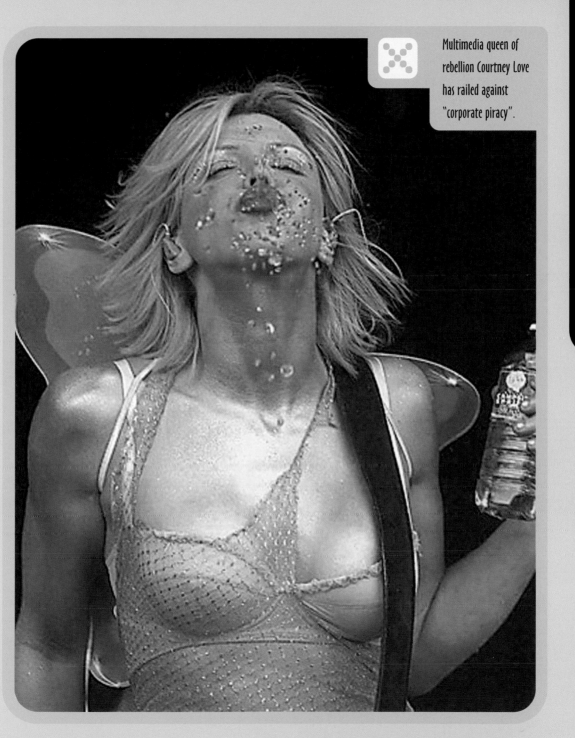

Multimedia queen of rebellion Courtney Love has railed against "corporate piracy".

anyone would be able to make your music sound the same as you. If you are truly paranoid, however, you can always take the traditional foolproof step of posting a copy of your music to yourself. When you receive the package, LEAVE IT UNOPENED and store it somewhere for safe keeping. This can provide you with cast-iron evidence that you produced a piece of music on a certain date. Even if it's unlikely to ever be necessary, it is a valid method of protection, which for the cost of a few stamps might make you sleep a little better at night.

The Record Contract

Traditionally, record contracts have consisted of three main areas of agreement: the ADVANCE

Motown founder Berry Gordy.

represents the money paid to the artist up front; the POINTS refer to the royalties or share of the profits that goes to the artist; and the COMMITMENT details what the company is contractually obligated to do on the artist's behalf. There was a time when these words could be taken quite literally: advance meant money for the artist to spend as he wanted, points was a simple percentage, and commitment meant that the artist had a career of some duration. This is no longer the case.

A label's budget for a record used to include separately allocated portions for recording (including studios and equipment), promotion and an advance on which the artist could live until the cash from their records came rolling in. All too often today, the budget IS the advance, which to all intents and purposes is the entire deal. As a one-off payment, the advance must cover EVERY expense incurred. End of story. This puts the burden of responsibility on the artist for dividing up that sum and making sure that it lasts long enough to pay for food and rent for a few years to come.

The concept of royalties is probably the most poorly understood aspect of the music world. It is SUPPOSED to mean a share of the profits, but in practice this is only a very loose definition. The price of a record in a shop (the RETAIL PRICE) is usually about twice what the record company receives (the DEALER PRICE). This money received for records sold must first go towards paying back EVERY PENNY of what the record company has spent on production, manufacture, the artist's advance, promotion, postage stamps, over-priced business lunches... and anything else that could reasonably be considered a cost. From what's left, the artist might expect to get 8 or 9 percentage points. From this figure, the artist will have to pay his band, manager and all other operating expenses.

Furthermore, an understanding of any royalty tabulation is almost certainly subject to further fine print somewhere else within the contract. Even accomplished lawyers and accountants have been defeated by clever "legalese" hiding an obscure detail. (Still fancy being your own lawyer?)

Commitment is the usual term for the record company's future plans regarding an artist's career. In this context, terms such as "three-album deal" were once commonplace and had some genuine meaning. This is sadly no longer true. Such carrots-on-a-stick exist only to tempt the uninformed. It's true to say that some contracts do refer to future albums. You may be offered a deal that uses such language as "the company is committed/obligated to release three albums over a five-year period". DO NOT BELIEVE IT. The outcome is likely to depend on a simple fact. If the first record does well for you and the company, you are very likely to be given another release; if it fails, you are unlikely to get any further releases regardless of any clauses in your contract. Either the fine print will let the company off, or they will simply ignore their commitment and expect you to be too poor to sue them – which, of course, you will be. It may sound cynical and mean, but that's the politics of the music industry.

The Product

Let's start with one of the great myths of the music business: THE VAST MAJORITY OF NEW ARTISTS WILL NOT BE SIGNED AFTER HAVING SENT IN A "DEMO" TAPE. In fact, the traditional demo – a roughly recorded demonstration of what the artist could sound like if produced properly – no longer exists in the same way. Three main factors have undermined this old institution:

1. The predominance of self-produced dance music, which is largely dependent on a sound created at the moment it was recorded. Record companies know they cannot recreate these sounds even if they really want to, and so they rarely bother trying.

2. Technology and computer-based recording systems have brought the quality of home recordings up towards the standards of high-priced professional studios. These days the vast majority of tapes and CDs sent out to record companies have hardly any hiss, rattle or hum (unless it's intentional).

German producer Giorgio Moroder pioneered the idea of the 12-inch "maxi-single" in the 1970s.

3. Why would a company bother to pay for re-recording when they don't need to? The labels have actually now arrived at the situation they always wanted to be in. Turning a demo into a releasable record has always been a risky business. For any number of reasons, thousands of artists have proved incapable of delivering the promise of their initial demos. With thousands of CD-quality recordings arriving at company offices every month, why not just sign and release the good ones and forget about the rest? And that, with a few exceptions, is largely what record companies do these days.

Pressing and Distribution

In truth, the modern record deal should really be called a "P and D" (pressing and distribution) deal. So if record companies aren't actually recording, then what are they doing? The answer is that they are duplicating and selling. Your master tape is turned into hundreds, thousands or millions of CDs, cassettes and records. It is distributed to retail shops and marketed in a variety of ways. That's it. In fact, whether or not they are labelled as such, these days very few record contracts are not for "P and D" deals.

Licensing

Similar to a "P and D" deal is a LICENSING agreement, where the company merely hires your music for a specific period of time. In this situation, an artist stands to make the best possible profit but disadvantages are many. For example, advances are likely to be small and so without an infrastructure to run a proper business, artists are less likely to do well out of such an arrangement.

Budget

The size of budgets on offer these days rarely seems to reflect reality. Even if the record company acknowledges that you are delivering fully-fledged masters ready for pressing, rarely is an artist paid enough to cover those costs. While companies routinely refer to their own recording budgets of up to £100,000 or more, a deal for a finished album could easily bring in 10 percent of that figure. While these companies will not balk at paying £1000/day for studios for their own jobs and services, a deal for a single might be less than that figure for everything.

Part of the problem is the perennial gap between the record companies' knowledge of how to sell records and their knowledge of how to make them. Few insiders understand even the basic techniques, not to mention the time and sweat involved. And a further problem is the ever-descending financial "bottom line", which continues to worsen each year.

Initially for all aspiring artists, the key is to produce and perfect your own album before even going to the companies. As this book shows you, it is now possible to create an entire album on a shoestring budget, and yet still equal the technical standards of a major-label record made with a thousand times that budget. The companies know this and therefore expect such technical brilliance in every prospective project offered to them. As always, there can be no deal without a "hit record". But there might be no deal even WITH a hit record. The risk of the budget is all yours.

Access

Getting your music heard by the right people is an obvious ingredient of success. A lot can surely depend on being in the right place at the right time, but there are things that you can do to create your own fortune:

1. SHOWCASES

In the past, "talent nights" have been known to connect musicians with record companies. As in real estate, location is everything. A gig in a fashionable club or at a music convention

For over 30 years, BBC radio DJ John Peel has heroically championed the obscure.

may attract the right audience, while a back woods venue is probably worth viewing as just a gig for the money or the experience.

2. RADIO

As the commercial radio world continues to expand, the number of listeners for any particular station declines. Inevitably this means that a single play on radio is less likely to create the same level of buzz than it once might have done. There is, however, a lot to be learned from hearing yourself and your music on the air – and the possibility of someone useful hearing you is quite real. So it's always worth sending records to appropriate radio DJs and their producers.

3. CLUBS

For dance music hopefuls, this is always a worthwhile route. Sending vinyl 12-inch records to club DJs and to dance and DJ magazines can yield unexpected results. The nature of DJing is that new and unknown records are always sought-after and desirable. While the better-known DJs may have hundreds of new records to screen each week, many will take the trouble to listen to nearly all of them (which is more than can be said for most record company A&R men). The unpredictable nature of dance music, and the ever-increasing influence of DJs, also allows for a one-off club-chart entry or club play to grow into a sizeable national hit.

Aside from such hit-or-miss tips, there isn't much an artist can do other than using any connections he has. But these days, networking can come in the most unlikely packages: lawyers, accountants, secretaries, personal assistants, club owners, DJs, other musicians, recording studio owners, equipment makers and dealers. Anyone who may come into contact with the employees or scouts of record companies may be helpful. So always carry a copy of your music with you and be prepared to give away as many copies as you can to potentially useful contacts.

It may seem like a depressing picture, but very little of this is new. The music business has always been a long-shot gamble. Record companies have always been money factories. Deals have always been heavily weighted in favour of the already-rich. But pop music has also always been the same: inspirationally brilliant and depressingly awful. The secret, as ever, is knowledge. Most people who fail come down at the first hurdle or don't even fill out the entry form. Success is 5% genius and 95% turning up.

Clubs such as DTPM at London's Fabric — shown here with DJ Miguel Pellitero at the decks — have become an obvious starting point for many hit records.

Cyber Cottage Industry

on peoplesound.com

Franc
Nederlan
Espa
Italia

peoplesound.com

Type in the name of an artist you like
and discover new music to match...

Radiohe: Search

Explore...

the definitive source of
great new music online
from thousands of quality
artists.

Charts & Reviews
Top 20
Editors Choice
Genre Charts
Latest Site Arrivals
Judge Jules
Official UK Album Chart
Official UK Singles Chart

News

Radio

My Jukebox

Offers

Labels & Music Partners

For Artists

Music Alert
Web Music for Beginners
A to Z Index

Genre of the month:
ndie ▶

Band of the day ▶

Choose Genre
Pop
Dance
Rock
Indie
Urban
Hip Hop
Classical
Global
New age
Jazz
Blues & Country
Folk
Reggae
Specialist

View all genres

NASH

World Exclusive
Freshly laid soul-funk and tight tune

Angelique
Unique pop with a warm heart... ▶

The Official UK Charts
Is Rui still ruling the roost? ▶

Nude Dimensions
A sassy and seductive floor worker...

Find a peoplesound artist   !Del   Searc

The Internet, and in particular the World Wide Web, is very probably the most significant development in human communication since Gutenberg invented the printing press over 500 years ago. Out there (among the pornographers, white supremacists, ranters, gamblers and midnight ramblers) lies a fantastic resource for musicians and music technologists.

Friends and Teachers: Bulletin Boards and User Groups

Because the Web has always been about sharing information, there have always been virtual forums where like-minded people could exchange ideas. These forums were called Bulletin Board Services (BBS), where messages could be posted and then answered. User Groups are BBSs set up by manufacturers, enthusiastic users, or hosted by a publications and magazines. These forums can be extremely helpful both for "newbies" and experienced professionals who are looking for general advice, comparing working methods, or trying to solve a specific problem that someone else may have already overcome.

Freeware and Shareware

The Web is also a fantastic resource for software downloads. If you are a registered user of a particular type of software program, you can download the latest updates as soon as they became available. This saves time waiting for updates to arrive in the post and you can get them at any time of the day or night. There are also demo versions available so you can "try before you buy". There are also many useful Freeware and Shareware programs available. Freeware programs are, as the name suggests, available for download at no cost. Shareware is also available at no cost, on the proviso that, if you like it and find it useful, you can register it for a nominal fee (usually less than £20). Although many Shareware users never pay up, remember that supporting the author of a good piece of software may give them the chance to use their talents to develop another equally useful application.

Virtual Jammin': The Rocket Network and Virtual Recording Studios

The Rocket Network was set up in 1995, initially, to enable real-time group playing over the Web using MIDI. This was limited, however, by the fact that MIDI carries no information regarding the sounds being used. In the last year or so, however, Rocket has increased its bandwidth to enable audio tracks to be transferred. This means that, having downloaded and installed the free Rocket Control software; you can actually "jam" with someone on the other side of the world.

The Rocket Network basically consists of a series of "virtual recording studios" set up on the Internet. These studios can be public – open to anyone who wants to join in and work on a track – or private, where someone has control over who is allowed to come into the studio and the ownership of whatever is created there.

There are three pieces of software needed to use this system:

- Rocket Control. This looks like a little "chat" window, but is in fact the brain which interconnects different MIDI/audio software.

- A web browser such as Internet Explorer or Netscape Navigator. This will show you who is in the studio, and which projects are being worked on.

- An audio application with RocketPower, such as Logic Platinum or ProTools.

Rocket network web servers co-ordinate a master arrangement of audio and MIDI parts shared by each user in the studio. Users can post their recorded tracks to the studio through RocketControl and any RocketPower-equipped audio software. Each post automatically updates the master arrangement and distributes the new parts to the studio participants. Whenever you enter a studio in which there is a project in progress, the most up-to-date arrangement is downloaded into your MIDI/audio sequencer. You can then add your own parts and, when you're satisfied, send them back to the studio.

This is real-time collaboration, but not real-time streaming of the media. This means that you're not

Britney Spears is more profitable than all the web-based record sellers put together.

Is Home Surfing Killing Music?

Don't forget that the most important change in the music business has been that of scale. Shipments of CDs are expected to break the one billion mark for the first time in 2000 (that figure is an increase from 940 million in 1999). Total shipments of CDs, DVDs and vinyl albums are likely to exceed $15 billion. This is twice the level of 1990 and loads more than in 1970. Many, many more records are released today than ever before. This year will see the release of more than 30,000 in the US alone – that's about ten times as many as in 1990.

Such numbers obviously create intense competition, but they also make scoring a major-label record deal more significant than ever before. The marketing muscle of a multinational corporation and its ability to secure wide radio and video exposure are vital if an artist is to be heard above the clamourous noise of new records. Word-of-mouth continues to be a helpful form of advertising, but it is now all-but-defeated by the mathematics of the business.

The Internet presents a possible solution to this problem, but as yet it's not quite clear just what that solution may be. The major labels are certainly concerned about the potential threat. Web-based free music site Napster.com has registered more than 20 million users, but none of them has paid a penny for the privilege.

actually playing together over the Internet at the same time (the bandwidth requirements for such practice would be prohibitive) but just overdubbing new parts as the arrangement develops. It does, however, open up great opportunities for musical collaboration. It may also go some way toward dispelling the stereotype of the geeky computer musician working alone in his or her bedroom.

In contrast to that success, the site MP3.com has albums available by more than 60,000 pop music artists, and yet only sell about 26,000 albums a month. For all its hype as the future of music, MP3.com has not yet sold as much IN TOTAL as Britney Spears sold on the day she released her last album. For all the fuss, the major labels are sleeping well at night.

Despite this David and Goliath scenario, the major labels are keeping up a strong fight. Any thrill of victory is certain to be fleeting however, as other file-exchange applications and services have since ridden the coat tails of Napster's infamy. Scour.com, Gnutella and Freenet have all enjoyed plenty of free international publicity courtesy of Napster and the major labels. The newer systems are unlike Napster, however, as they do not rely on a single centralized server. It appears that there would be no way to shut down Freenet without shutting down the entire Internet. In essence, Freenet uses the Internet as a giant communal hard drive. Users download the Freenet code and agree to allocate a certain number of megabytes on their hard drives to the storage of Freenet files. Any sort of information can then be stored on the participating computers. If Freenet is truly immune to the injunctions and penalties of any court, perhaps it's only a matter of time before the whole world's system will be forced into a major rethink of the way copyright is enforced.

Some labels have reacted quickly by creating "virtual record shops" of their own, but rumours of a plan to charge $3.49 per song have only added fuel to the fire. Rumours also abound that the labels will soon announce "copy-protected" CDs, but – apart from the technical challenge of successfully achieving this – there remains the problem of the billions of pirated CDs already sold. As with most issues of security, the real answers will only be known long after the battle is finished.

From His Master's Voice to His Master's Music

As we all expected, the Internet has become the focus for selling pop music. Many websites exist for just this purpose, and many more use music sales as an added attraction. Indeed, few "youth-oriented" websites are without some kind of CD or downloadable music offer. While these sites may seem to be "virtual record shops", the reality is that they effectively offer very little real choice and tend to lead the buyer towards certain records that suit the aims of the record company.

The first type of web record shop is the dedicated site, such as PeopleSound.com or MP3.com. These sites sprang up early on and caught the imagination of many first-time surfers. This is the basis on which they work:

1. You log on and complete the "contract". This offers you a web page of your own on which you can load a "soundbite" of your music to be available for prospective buyers to audition. Profit on all sales is split between artist and website. This can be anything from a third or a half of the purchase-price to a sliver of the "profit".

2. You upload your music to the site via MP3 or other Freeware languages.

3. You sit back and watch your own web page appear inside the site.

4. There is no form of "exclusivity" on most of these sites – you can sign up to as many different ones as you like.

This may seem quite straight-forward and fair, and to a large extent it is. There is, however, a downside. Most of these sites have now been

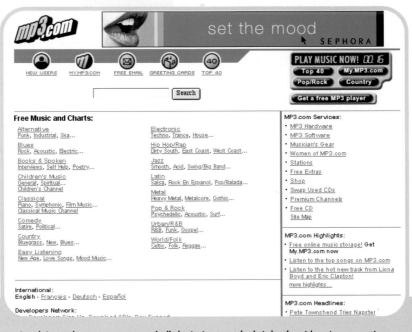

Trend-setting music websites such as mp3.com are gradually beginning to settle their battles with major corporations.

around for quite a while and many musicians have signed up. This means that the site may have more than a hundred-thousand artists on their books and nearly as many pages for buyers to wade through. How many people have the time needed to audition so many records? Do would-be buyers judge a record by its cover? How can a person make a choice out of such a vast collection? While this may strike some as being not very different from a huge megastore of records, others fear that most buyers are simply relying on the site's own charts. These *might* be compiled by someone who actually listens to all of the songs on the site, but more often than not they are simply lists of the tracks which are being bought the most.

Welcome to "Clickola"

Throughout the last 50 years of record charts, the scourge of the music business was a practice known

as "payola". This was when certain record companies would "buy" their records onto the radio station's playlist through illicit payments directly to a radio DJ or producer. While this was strictly illegal, the reality was that the pop charts were effectively controlled by this "insider crime". Well, the more things change, the more they stay the same. Many of these websites have been accused of being under a similar influence. This can be true when a company employs people to download a certain song so many times and so artificially creates a hit on the site's "chart". It causes many unwitting buyers to naturally migrate toward a song that they wouldn't otherwise have noticed. It can make a song dominate a chart for undeservedly long periods. This practice is known as "clickola". As yet, there is no known cure.

Another form of web-based approach to music sales is the "pick 'n' mix" CD-by-post. This is when you peruse a web-site's list of songs and assemble your very own audio CD, which is then sent to you. The list of available songs is usually very familiar and this can be very appealing to casual surfers. The problems are usually with quality, price or even reliability. Sometimes, the site will wait a long time before producing your CD – to see how many others want the same one – thereby cutting overheads. Some sites may be pirating the songs from other records. Again, no cure is currently available.

There has been a lot of hype about record companies using certain sites (usually their own) as virtual "showcases" for new talent. Certainly, the recent culling of A&R staff in London would seem to support this. The problem, however, remains the same: how to choose from hundreds of thousands of offerings. The record companies are not likely to solve this soon. In the meantime, aspiring bands can assume that the old routes of sending CD's in the post or via a contact, and playing live at notable venues, remain the best bet.

Consumers seem set to be plunged into a difficult position. High street retailers are increasingly feeling the pressure of net-music and some have given ultimatums to the companies on the lines of "help us or we leave the trade". For CD and vinyl lovers, this will inevitably mean less choice and higher prices. For Web-lovers, the future is bliss. For music fans in general, these are uncertain times.

The Law of the Internet

The High Noon of Cyberspace is nearly upon us. Lawlessness and chaos rein. Sheriff Government watches from behind the front window of his station while The Law of the Wild West plays out its own bloody storyline. The whole town is crying out for him to act but, so far, he looks helpless.

In every area of on-line life, uncertainty is norm. In book publishing, even Stephen King awaits day-to-day news of developments before deciding whether to "publish" the next chapter of his book on the Web. In the retail trade, every major player looks anxiously at his rivals before taking baby steps into the darkness of "e-commerce". The pioneers have fallen more than they've succeeded. The medical profession can't decide whether to look to the establishment or the pioneers for support in on-line practice.

The same confusion rules for the music world. Everyone seems happy and certain about a musician's right to make money from his music, but everyone also seems to be happy enough to download whatever music they can without paying for it. Napster.com and mp3.com remain the focus of attention in this area, each case throwing up questions that cannot easily be answered. But the biggest and most obvious question is about piracy. Is "music-sharing" on the Web the same thing as piracy? How is this any different to lending CDs to friends? Is there a difference between borrowing a CD from a friend and actually taping the album onto a cassette? If the music world accepted years ago that home taping was difficult to stop, then surely this new alternative is equally impossible to stop?

The major labels know that there is no "tape police". They have accepted that a certain amount of profit would inevitably be lost to home taping. But this did not stop the business of selling records and nor did it stop the business of selling tape machines. The majors simply built-in the costs and carried on. As in life, even if you can't stop the onion from making you cry, you can still make dinner.

Napster and mp3.com

For the time being, expect quite a few "anti-cry" methods to delay the meal. Inevitably, the first port of call for the record companies is The Law. The case against Napster.com has already provided a few thrills. The combined might of the record industry initially won an injunction to shut the site down, but before anything could happen, the site won an

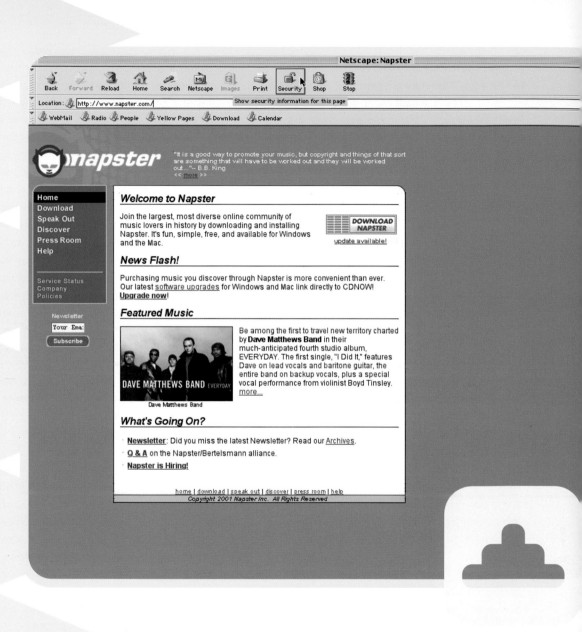

Netscape: Napster

Back | Forward | Reload | Home | Search | Netscape | Images | Print | Security | Shop | Stop

Location: http://www.napster.com/

Show security information for this page

WebMail | Radio | People | Yellow Pages | Download | Calendar

napster

"It is a good way to promote your music, but copyright and things of that sort are something that will have to be worked out and they will be worked out..."-- B.B. King
<< more >>

- Home
- Download
- Speak Out
- Discover
- Press Room
- Help

Service Status
Company
Policies

Newsletter
Your Ema:
Subscribe

Welcome to Napster

Join the largest, most diverse online community of music lovers in history by downloading and installing Napster. It's fun, simple, free, and available for Windows and the Mac.

DOWNLOAD NAPSTER
update available!

News Flash!

Purchasing music you discover through Napster is more convenient than ever. Our latest software upgrades for Windows and Mac link directly to CDNOW! **Upgrade now!**

Featured Music

Dave Matthews Band

Be among the first to travel new territory charted by **Dave Matthews Band** in their much-anticipated fourth studio album, EVERYDAY. The first single, "I Did It," features Dave on lead vocals and baritone guitar, the entire band on backup vocals, plus a special vocal performance from violinist Boyd Tinsley. more...

What's Going On?

- **Newsletter**: Did you miss the latest Newsletter? Read our Archives.
- **Q & A** on the Napster/Bertelsmann alliance.
- **Napster is Hiring!**

home | download | speak out | discover | press room | help
Copyright 2001 Napster Inc. All Rights Reserved

After a "David and Goliath" battle, free music music website Napster.com has finally jumped into bed with the corporate world.

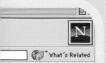

appeal and remained open. The endgame is still a long way off.

The case against mp3.com was so strong initially that three of the four majors accepted a settlement offered by mp3.com. One company, however, would not accept any settlement – Universal went on to fight their case and won more than $100 million in "damages" for estimated lost profit. In the end, it is likely that this and other similar cases will change on appeal,

Such an event may be a development of technology. If a workable "copy-prohibit' system became available to manufacturers, the majors would surely jump aboard. The biggest problem would be all the old CDs and records that remain out there and copyable. It's clear that the majors make a lot of money out of old recordings and they clearly want to keep doing so.

More likely, the outcome will be a shift in business practices and attitudes. Just as the video recorder presented a fatal threat to the movie companies in the early 1980s (at the time many predicted the end of the cinema as we know it), the World Wide Web has surely been similarly misunderstood. As the world gradually adapts to this mighty new tool of instant communication, so the business community will inevitably discover numerous ways to exploit it. Perhaps the immediate problem lies in the format; maybe MP3 itself is ill suited to protection. Perhaps the problem is in volume; maybe when the world music market includes substantial numbers in Africa and the Far East, then the amount lost in piracy will become relatively too small to worry about. Perhaps, like the Supermarket trade, the profit margin of the music business naturally exists at about 2% rather than at the current "get-rich-quick" levels that the major record labels have traditionally been accustomed.

WebMail Radio People Yellow Pages Download Calendar

napster

| **Copyright Policy** | Terms of Use | Privacy Policy |

Home
Download
Speak Out
Discover
Press Room
Help

Service Status
Company
Policies

Napster Copyright Policy

Napster is an integrated browser and communications system provided by Napster, Inc., to enable musicians and music fans to locate bands and music available in the MP3 music format. The MP3 files that you locate using Napster are not stored on Napster's servers. Napster does not, and cannot, control what content is available to you using the Napster browser. Napster users decide what content to make available to others using the Napster browser, and what content to download. Users are responsible for complying with all applicable federal and state laws applicable to such content, including copyright laws.

Napster respects copyright law and expects our users to do the same. Unauthorized copying, distribution, modification, public display, or public performance of copyrighted works is an infringement of the copyright holders' rights. You should be aware that some MP3 files may have been created or distributed without copyright owner authorization. As a condition to your account with Napster, you agree that you will not use the Napster service to infringe the intellectual property rights of others in any way. Napster will terminate the accounts of users who are repeat infringers of the copyrights, or other intellectual property rights, of others. In addition, Napster reserves the right to terminate the account of a user and to block use of the Napster service permanently upon any single infringement of the rights of others in conjunction with use of the Napster service, or if Napster believes that user conduct is harmful to the interests of Napster, its affiliates, or other users, or for any other reason in Napster's sole discretion, with or without cause.

In accordance with the Digital Millennium Copyright Act of 1998 (the text of which may be found on the U.S. Copyright Office web site at http://lcweb.loc.gov/copyright/), Napster will respond expeditiously to claims of copyright infringement committed using the Napster service that are reported to Napster's "Designated Copyright Agent" identified below. If you are a copyright owner, or authorized to act on behalf of an owner of the copyright or of any exclusive right under the copyright, please report your notice of infringement by completing the following notice form and delivering it to the Designated Copyright Agent:

NOTICE OF ALLEGED INFRINGEMENT OF COPYRIGHT

ending up with smaller amounts being awarded or even defeat, but the struggle in the courts is sure to continue for some .

In time, the music industry will see the light at the end of the tunnel. Even if it emerges at the other end looking rather different.

A Basic Recording Session

Step One: "What are we going to do today?"

This question is all too often overlooked. Many people find themselves hours into a session before stopping to ask themselves "what ARE we doing?" It's true that wonderful things can sometimes come from spontaneous and instinctive improvisation. It's also true that over-analysis can ruin a vibe and makes things feel contrived. But, more often, a little method to the madness can save a lot of time. The aim is usually to write and record a song, but it may also be to outline or "demo" song, create a big drum track, or simply to audition a singer. Whatever it is, stay focused.

Step Two: "Where shall we begin?"

Assuming that the session is a fresh one – that the aim is to create a new song from scratch – it pays to be clear about your starting point. Without a doubt, the most popular place to get going is to start with a drum track. Most people seem to feel better about life after a groove is going. This can be done quite quickly by using a drum loop, such as a sampled drum pattern lifted from a record. More traditional musicians often prefer to start with a piano sound in order to try to find a seed of inspiration. A singer might like to begin a session by recording the voice, singing a line or two, and then experimenting with other sounds on top.

Step Three: Set the framework

You can't do anything before you decide on a tempo. This may not be a conscious decision, but it will always take place. A ballad might be 85 beats per minute (BPM) while a dance tune is more likely to be between 120-140 BPM. It can be a good idea to question your own regular working methods. If you normally use the computer to sequence your sounds drums and play them back from a drum machine, it might give you a fresh perspective to program the drums on the drum machine. If you normally play the bass first, try, for example, starting with a piano part. As for interaction, it's astonishing to think how many people never bother trying to create a set-up where it's possible for two people to "jam" on two instruments simultaneously. With a few notable exceptions, two minds are usually better than one.

Step Four: Prepare to record immediately

The best ideas are always the ones that get away. The shrewdest people are those who have a system set-up for recording straight away. If you are using a computer-sequencer, it pays to create a track, set the quantize, assign the MIDI channel and set up a "loop" (or whatever else you like to have ready) BEFORE YOU BEGIN TO PLAY.

One some sequencers (such as Logic), a "fail-safe" recording buffer is always in operation. This means that everything played on the master keyboard is always being recorded. In this way, the last performance can always be retrieved by simultaneously hitting and holding the SHIFT and RETURN keys. Thus, each time someone plays something brilliant and says "that sounded good, what did I just do?", the performance will have been (secretly) recorded into the temporary hidden buffer from which it can be easily retrieved. That can be a real life-saver.

Step Five: Getting a vibe and overdubbing

A great hook is only a great hook until it has a context, so after the basic idea is in place it needs quick development. These initial "seeds" can now be used as a means of generating more ideas. Experiment widely but quickly. Don't spend time cleaning up details – you can do that later. You need just enough to capture the flavour of whatever is happening. If somebody is eager to try out some idea that is already forming in his head, do it before it becomes clouded both by time and by other people's subsequent ideas.

Step Six: Adding form and structure

After the initial rush of ideas and performances has been played out, take a few minutes to think and talk about "The Big Picture". Try to arrange the song in your head and then put it together on your sequencer's Arrange Window. Experiment with different structures. Use this time to free your mind. At this point, an unorthodox introduction, middle-eight or ending might give you that edge, so don't always lock yourself inside the standard "verse-bridge-chorus" way of thinking.

Step Seven: Is it time for vocals or solo instruments?

There are whole genres of music that never use vocals, so for many people singing is merely an optional extra. If you do turn to vocals at this stage, remember that the music you've recorded is still malleable and re-writable – if necessary, you can adapt the music to fit the vocals. If you don't use vocals at all, you might want to consider using a solo instrument. Keep an open mind as to what instruments are suitable for your music. Ask yourself if you know anyone who could come in and jam over the tune?

Step Eight: Analyse and reconsider

This penultimate step should ideally come after a period of reflection – at least after a night's rest. If not, take a break. Use this time to clean your mind's palate so that you can return to the session with a fresh attitude. Re-focus on the song with a new perspective, perhaps as a harsh editor or a fierce critic. Use this last opportunity to tame any over-indulgences or to excite any boring bits.

Step Nine: Mix

Ideally, you should enter "mix mode" only when you're certain that the recording is finished. Here you should devote all of your time to making the best possible sum of the finished parts. In reality, most people will still find at least one more part to record in the mix. But when this happens try to keep it short and sweet. Don't lose your "overall" perspective – THAT IS SO VITAL AT THIS LATE STAGE IN THE PRODUCTION. If you find yourself getting seriously bogged down in further recording it probably indicates that you were not actually ready to mix in the first place, so you should postpone it until another day. If you can complete the extra bits reasonably quickly, then try to regain your mix-mode mentality as quickly as possible. Forget the details of what you've just recorded and keep asking yourself the ultimate question "WHAT'S THE DIFFERENCE BETWEEN AN EXCELLENT FINISHED RECORDING AND WHAT I'M NOW HEARING?"

Step Ten: Make yourself a safety copy and a personal copy

After the final mix has been recorded onto your "mastering" format you must be sure to listen back to your mix FROM THE MASTER. When you are sure that the mix is as brilliant as you can manage, make a copy of the master. If it's on DAT, use a second machine to make a copy. If it's on the computer, make a back-up copy on hard disk or CD-R. (Even better, make TWO copies – you can never be too secure in this area.)

APPENDIX B
PCs for Idiots

Personal computers come in two basic forms: the all-in-one "laptop" and the more common desk-top models consisting of a separate processor unit (the "Big Box"), monitor, keyboard and mouse.

1. Turning on the power

As this is easily the most embarrassing thing to not know, it's probably the ideal place to start. Regular desk-tops have two "on" buttons to deal with. The master power control (the "on/off" switch) will be found somewhere on the processor unit. Once that has been engaged, the PC can be switched on by pressing and holding down the circular button on the top right-hand corner of the keyboard. You will

also need to check that the monitor's own power switch has already been turned on.

Once you are aware of some activity, the PC is likely to take about three minutes before it is fully operational. Most (although by no means all) PC users run their applications through one of the Microsoft Windows operating systems. If loaded, this will automatically run by itself when you power up. The following tips all assume that you are using a version of Windows.

2. The Mouse

A PC mouse has two buttons. It is quite possible (and acceptable) to use only the left-hand mouse button. Every function of every application is available using just this button and the keyboard. The "right" button can be used for shortcuts.

3. The Desktop.

All icons that appear on the Windows desktop will always be directly accessible. If you recognize the icon of the desired program, simply double-click on it and the application will open.

4 The START MENU

The little box in the lower left corner of the screen is the START MENU. If you click and hold on this button, the START box will expand vertically and display your START MENU. This is divided into three sections. The top part will have a few quick routes to often-used programs.

The middle section of the START menu contains the "guts" of the PC. The first entry is called PROGRAMS. This contains every application on your computer. Position the mouse on the small arrow just to the right of the word PROGRAMS and a large list ("drop-down menu") opens vertically. To open any one of these programs, drag the mouse over the program name and hit the left mouse button. Beneath PROGRAMS is an entry called FAVOURITES. This is another drop-down menu list but only contains functions that the user wants to keep handy for easy access. This is followed by DOCUMENTS which is also used for handy access, but this time only to files created by programs – for example, letters written using Microsoft Word. Below that you will find SETTINGS, which is used to customize the appearance and functionality of the computer. Next down is FIND, which is used for locating a lost file inside the computer. The final two choices are HELP (a brief guide to the PC) and RUN (which is rarely used these days).

The bottom section of the START MENU has two choices. LOG OFF allows you to switch off Windows and return to DOS (the PC's "real" operating system). This is of little use to most people. The final entry is SHUT DOWN. Click here and you will be given four further choices: STANDBY sends the computer to sleep; SHUT DOWN is the ONE AND ONLY way you should switch off your PC; RESTART reboots the PC; RESTART IN MS DOS MODE restarts the computer but does not automatically run Windows.

5. Connections

The standard PC was never designed for music applications. There are no MIDI sockets. There is no PLAY or STOP button. There is no jack socket for a keyboard or a microphone. Therefore, making music on a PC requires some adaptor boxes. Each music application has its own required additions, so you'll need to consult the manual to figure out what's needed up front.

6. Saving your music

Make your plans in advance for how you will save your work – you MUST know how you will be doing this before the crucial moment of truth arrives. Of course, you will be saving your sounds and sequences into the hard disk of the PC. This is easily and quickly done. The upper left-hand corner of all program screens have a FILE menu. Here you will find the SAVE and SAVE AS commands. The first time you save your song use SAVE AS. This will allow you to name the file and choose the place you wish to save it. All subsequent saves can be made using the SAVE command (which can be done instantly and frequently by hitting CONTROL and "S"). If you are saving onto the hard disk, then begin by making a NEW FOLDER and giving it a suitable name. You can then save everything from your current session into that folder.

If you are saving only to the hard disk, then remember to periodically save onto a floppy disk, CD or second hard drive as well. Here is a special warning: LIKE ALL STORAGE MEDIA, HARD DISKS HAVE A FINITE LIFE – ONE DAY YOUR DRIVE WILL IRREPARABLY CRASH. IF YOU DON'T HAVE SOME KIND OF BACKUP YOUR DATA WILL BE LOST.

7. Turning off the power

Make sure you have saved your work. Open the START MENU and click on SHUT DOWN. Choose SHUT DOWN by clicking in the little white circle and make sure the black dot has appeared in that circle. Then click in OK. The PC will tell you that "WINDOWS IS SHUTTING DOWN" and then that "IT'S NOW OK TO TURN OFF YOUR COMPUTER". You don't really need to turn off your computer – it's already "off enough" – but if you are using a separate screen you can switch that off now. That's it.

How to be a Mac Man

Released in 1984, the Apple Macintosh was the first commercially available computer to use a "desktop" screen layout. This quickly set a new standard for user-friendliness throughout the computer industry. Because of this, the Mac operating system has always been easy to use and so was quickly taken up by computer music enthusiasts and MIDI software developers in the USA.

Mac Hardware

Apple has produced many versions of the Macintosh over the years, each one capable of running MIDI sequencing programs. However, as this software has grown in complexity, only models from the G3 range onwards can be recommended to run the latest software.

Introduced in 1998, the original G3 was the link between earlier models and the modern stylized multi-coloured Macs. The "beige" G3 had the same type of desktop and mini-tower cases as their predecessors and also used similar connections. These included the ADB (Apple Desktop Buss) to connect the keyboard and mouse, two serial ports for printer and modem, and a SCSI interface to connect external storage devices. The next generation of G3s (the "Blue & Whites") abandoned these ports, replacing them with USB (Universal Serial Buss). This caused problems for a while, as third-party hardware and software manufacturers worked hard to incorporate these major changes. The current G4 now offers the best solution for serious audio applications, although iMacs, Powerbooks and iBooks can also provide a powerful platform for your music.

Mac Software

The most important piece of software for a Macintosh or any other computer is the OPERATING SYSTEM (OS). The OS is constantly being updated to introduce new functions and to provide support for new hardware. Mac OSX is a major redesign and has yet to be fully utilized by most music software designers. Mac OS 8.6 and OS 9.04 have proved to be the most stable of the versions for running most audio applications.

When you first switch on your Mac (by pushing the button at the top right-hand corner of the keyboard) you should see the smiling "Happy Mac" icon on the screen indicating that the OS is launching. A line of icons will gradually be displayed as the individual EXTENSIONS are loaded into the computer's RAM. Extensions are small software add-ons to the OS that are needed to run certain pieces of hardware or software. If you're running software that does not require a certain extension, you can turn it off using the EXTENSIONS MANAGER panel. This is accessible in CONTROL PANELS under the Apple drop-down menu at the top left of the screen.

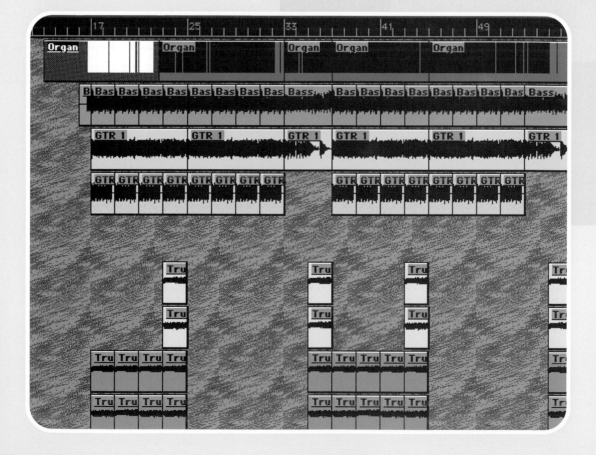

Making the Leap to Macintosh

Macintosh Memory

The Mac uses BLOCK MEMORY ALLOCATION instead of the DYNAMIC MEMORY ALLOCATION system used in Windows. This means that a specified BLOCK of memory is assigned to each program when it is open. You can check on the status by activating the FINDER (click on the icon in top right-hand corner of the screen) and clicking on the APPLE MENU (top left-hand corner of the screen) and choosing ABOUT THIS COMPUTER. This will show you the current memory allocation and usage of every currently open program (including the Mac OS).

Block memory allocation has its advantages and disadvantages. The main benefit is that the program doesn't have to share the memory and, as a result, the CPU doesn't have to interrupt to handle the memory allocation. This means that your program will run just as fast irrespective of how much RAM is being used (instead of slowing down as the RAM usage grows and more CPU is taken, as happens in Windows).

The only real disadvantage is that if you get a memory fragment caused by loading and unloading multiple programs, it may "frag" (or confuse) the OS. This will require you to either "force quit" (Command + Option + Escape), or to do a "forced reboot" (Command + Control + Restart [upper right corner]) to correct it.

How do you assign memory blocks to programs?
In this example, we'll alter the memory allocation for the ProTools program. Begin by finding the actual application file, which is usually located in the folder for the program. Open your PROTOOLS folder. Find what you think is the application – in this case it's just called PROTOOLS 5. Select it by clicking just once to highlight the icon (don't double-click or else that will start the program). Type Command + I (or choose GET INFO from the FILE menu). This will bring up the GET INFO Window. This tells you what kind of file you are looking at. If you have correctly selected the application, the first line of the window will read KIND: APPLICATION PROGRAM. In this case, you will see your memory allocation settings at the bottom of the window. The PREFERRED setting is the one that you need want to change. Type in a new number to allocate that portion of RAM to this program when it is opened. The next time you open the program it will automatically take that much memory. You can use this technique for any other application.

The Macintosh file system and the Finder are often seen as alien ideas to many Windows users. Every file on a Windows machine has a path that tells everything else that might need to know where everything is (*drive name\windows\user*). On a Mac, this information is stored in an invisible database that is continually updated as files are moved, trashed, copied or generally manipulated. Every drive contains such a file, which is called the DESKTOP FILE. This means is that you can rename drives, folder and files, relocate program folders and generally move things around in any way you like and it won't confuse the computer. This is because all new information is immediately updated in the Desktop File automatically. This is one of the major advantages of the Mac OS file system – it allows YOU to work in the way that YOU want to (not the way Bill Gates wants you to).

The Finder is a kind of equivalent to the Windows START MENU, although it's not as directly convenient. It displays the icon of the application currently in use in the top right-hand corner of the screen. As you've already seen, if you click on the icon it will display a list of all currently running applications. One of the things that most Mac beginners do, especially if they come from a PC environment, is to close applications by closing the window. On a Mac, this only closes the window – THE APPLICATION IS STILL RUNNING. You can tell this because the toolbar at the top of the screen still displays the menu items for the last application you had open.

To learn how this works, try to open any three applications at the same time. There are two ways to shuffle whatever is in the foreground – ACTIVE or INACTIVE. One way is to go to the Finder in the upper right corner of your screen and click and simply select which program you want to make active. If you watch the open windows on your screen as you select the different programs, the program's corresponding window jumps to the foreground and its toolbar pops up across the top of your screen. The Finder is where you get the standard Mac OS tools, such as EMPTY TRASH (under the SPECIAL menu), ERASE or INITIALIZE DISK, as well as ABOUT THIS COMPUTER under the Apple Menu (which changes to ABOUT THIS PROGRAM if you have a program in the foreground).

But, there is a much easier and intuitive way. Just click on the window you want to bring to the front. All the others will jump to the background and will appear "greyed out". If you arrange your windows so that they overlap, you will find that toggling through programs is as easy as clicking on any of them. Although this is very straightforward, it can also lead to window clutter, so take advantage of another unique Mac feature: Window Shade. The far right button on the top of the application window will scroll the window up leaving just the Title Bar in view. Clicking on the same button will restore the window to full size. As with Windows, you can resize or move around your windows in any way you wish. Keyboard shortcuts are listed beside the commands in the toolbar menus.

For more Macintosh information, bookmark http://www.macsurfer.com. This is far and away the BEST Macintosh web resource site.

Mac Troubleshooting

At a system level, Macs use many of the same elements as a PC. For example, users of PCs will recognize the features of the Macintosh Control Panel, which is accessed through the Apple Menu. Your printing, however, is performed through the Chooser (again, accessed through the Apple Menu). What PC users know as "Dlls" are EXTENSIONS in the Macintosh. Unlike PCs, these don't usually reside within their program's folder; instead they are held together in one place, the EXTENSIONS FOLDER that resides within the Mac's System Folder.

Most of the time, if you have a problem with your Mac it will be the result of a bad or conflicting extension. If after installing a new program you find that your Mac won't start up and just bombs out, do a "force restart" again (Command + Control + Restart) on the keyboard and hold down the Shift key until you see the EXTENSIONS OFF message. This will start up your Mac with the extensions switched off, allowing you to do a spot of troubleshooting.

The Extensions Manager

As one of the Control Panels, the EXTENSIONS MANAGER allows you to create sets containing activated and deactivated extensions. This can be extremely useful when troubleshooting. By paring down the extensions loaded you can easily identify those that have been corrupted. This is because when you deactivate the bad extension your Mac will be able to boot up in the normal way. For this reason it's always a good idea to have a specific set of extensions for different uses you may have for your Mac.

If you have an errant extension that keeps causing the system to "lockup" (or "freeze") here is a good approach to locating the culprit. After restarting with extensions off, go to the Extensions Manager (via the Apple Menu and Control Panels) and toggle half the extensions and Control Panels so that they are switched off. Now restart WITHOUT holding the Shift key. If you Mac boots successfully, then the bad extension must have been in the half you toggled off. Now you can start reactivating those extensions you switched off one at a time until you find the offending item.

Another item of maintenance is the Desktop File. Since it is being continually updated, it can easily become corrupted. The symptoms of this can range from oddly displaying icons to applications quitting unexpectedly. As a regular course of maintenance – perhaps about once every three weeks – it's a good idea to "rebuild" your Desktop File. To do this, restart whilst holding down the Command key and the Option key together until you see the message "Are you sure you want to rebuild the desktop on volume?" Hit the "OK" button. Mac OS will rebuild you a brand spanking new file directory.

Aliases

If you don't like having to click open various windows to get to your favourite everyday applications, make an "alias" of that application and then drop it into the Apple Menu folder within your System Folder. It will then show up in your Apple Menu making it as accessible as the Windows START MENU. (To create an alias, single-click on the application and then press Command + M.)

Useful Websites

http://www.nuendo.com	Information on Steinberg's PC audio workstation.
http://www.digidesign.com	For ProTools and related software and hardware.
http://www.emagic.de	For Logic MIDI/audio sequencer and recording information.
http://www.harmony-central.com	Outlet for an extraordinarily varied array of music products.
http://www.rocketnetwork.com	Virtual studio homepage.
http://www.tweakheadz.com	Good all-around MIDI site.
http://www.NemesysMusic.com	Homepage and information about the PC Virtual Geiger sampler.
http://tile.net/news/recaudiopro.html	Professional audio bulletin board.
http://www.musicplayer.com	Answers to questions for all musicians.
http://www.pure-mac.com	For all things related to Apple Macintosh.
http://www.info-mac.org	Updates and downloads for Apple Macintosh.
http://www.logicuser.net	E-Magic homepage.
http://www.gnutella.wego.com	Even better than Napster.com.
http://www.blackholemedia.com/macster	The Apple Macintosh version of Napster.com.
http://genres.mp3.com/music	MP3 artists page.
http://music.cnet.com	Downloads of MP3 files.
http://www.us.steinberg.net/home.nsf	Homepage for Steinberg's Cubase VST software.

APPENDIX F
Charts: Beats per Minute and Time Stretch

Beat Charts

This list shows the most effective delay times to use as a starting point to set on your delay effect. Starting with the tempo of your song (measured in beats per minute), try using any one (or two numbers simultaneously) in that row as delay times. These correct times will allow you to use high settings of delay "feedback" (or "spin") without creating a messy mix.

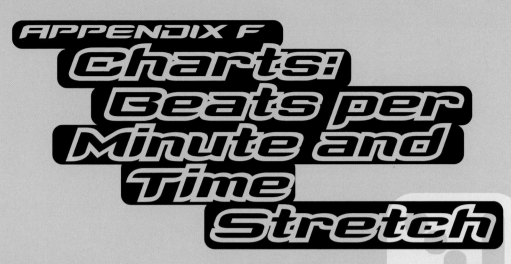

BPM	1/16	3/32	1/8	5/32	3/16	7/32	1/4	3/8	3/6	Milliseconds/bar	Frames/Beat (EBU)
70	214	321	428	535	642	749	857	1071	1285	3428	21.425
71	211	316	422	528	633	739	845	1056	1267	3380	21.125
72	208	312	416	520	624	728	833	1041	1249	3322	20.825
73	205	307	410	513	615	718	821	1026	1231	3284	20.525
74	202	303	405	506	607	708	810	1012	1215	3240	20.25
75	200	300	400	500	600	700	800	1000	1200	3200	20
76	197	295	394	493	591	690	789	986	1183	3156	10.725
77	194	292	389	486	584	681	779	973	1168	3118	19.475
78	192	288	334	480	576	672	769	961	1153	3076	19.225
79	189	284	379	474	569	664	759	948	1138	3018	18.975
80	187	281	375	469	562	656	750	937	1125	3000	18.75
81	186	277	370	462	555	647	740	925	1110	2960	18.5
82	102	274	365	456	540	639	731	913	1096	2924	10.275
83	180	270	361	451	541	631	722	902	1083	2888	18.05
84	178	267	357	446	535	624	714	892	1071	2856	17.85
85	176	264	352	440	528	616	705	881	1057	2820	17.625
86	174	261	348	435	522	609	697	871	1045	2788	17.425
07	172	250	344	430	515	602	609	061	1033	2750	17.225
88	170	255	340	425	510	595	681	851	1021	2724	17.025
89	168	262	337	421	505	589	674	842	1011	2696	16.85
90	166	249	333	416	499	582	666	832	999	2664	16.65
91	164	247	329	411	494	576	659	823	988	2636	16.3
92	183	244	326	407	489	570	652	815	978	2608	16.3
93	161	241	322	403	483	564	645	806	967	2580	16.125
94	159	239	319	398	478	558	638	797	957	2552	15.95
95	157	236	315	394	473	552	631	788	946	2524	15.775
96	156	234	312	290	488	546	625	781	937	2500	15.625
97	154	231	309	366	463	540	618	772	927	2472	15.45
98	153	229	306	382	459	535	612	765	918	2448	15.3
99	151	227	303	378	454	530	606	757	909	2427	15.15
100	150	225	300	375	450	525	600	750	900	2400	15
101	148	222	297	371	445	519	594	742	891	2376	14.85
102	147	220	294	367	441	514	588	735	882	2352	14.7
103	145	218	291	363	436	509	582	727	873	2328	14.55
104	144	216	288	360	432	504	576	720	864	2304	14.4
105	142	214	285	356	428	499	571	713	856	2284	14.275
106	141	212	283	353	424	495	566	707	849	2264	14.15
107	140	210	280	350	420	490	560	697	825	2240	13.875
108	138	208	277	346	416	485	555	693	832	2220	14.
109	137	206	275	343	412	481	550	687	825	2200	13.75

BPM	1/16	3/32	1/8	5/32	3/16	7/32	1/4	3/8	3/6	Milliseconds/bar	Frames/Beat (EBU)
110	136	204	272	340	408	476	545	681	817	2180	13.635
111	135	202	270	337	405	472	540	675	810	2160	13.5
112	133	200	267	334	401	468	535	668	802	2140	13.375
113	132	298	265	331	397	463	530	662	795	2129	13.25
114	131	197	263	328	394	460	526	657	789	2104	13.15
115	130	195	260	325	290	455	521	651	781	2084	13.025
116	129	193	258	323	287	452	517	646	775	2068	12.975
117	128	192	256	320	284	448	512	640	768	2048	12.8
118	127	190	254	317	381	444	508	635	762	2032	12.7
119	126	189	252	315	378	441	504	630	756	2018	12.6
120	125	187	250	312	375	437	500	625	750	2000	12.5
121	123	185	247	308	371	433	495	618	742	1980	12.375
122	122	184	245	306	368	429	491	613	736	1964	12.275
123	121	182	243	304	365	426	487	608	730	1948	12.175
124	120	181	241	301	362	422	483	603	724	1932	12.075
125	120	180	240	300	360	420	480	600	720	1920	12
126	119	178	238	297	357	416	476	595	714	1904	11.9
127	118	177	236	295	354	413	472	590	708	1888	11.8
128	117	175	234	292	351	409	468	583	702	1872	11.7
129	116	174	232	290	348	406	465	581	697	1860	11.625
130	115	172	230	288	345	403	461	576	691	1844	11.525
131	114	171	229	286	343	400	458	572	687	1832	11.45
132	113	170	227	283	340	397	454	567	681	1818	11.35
133	112	169	225	281	338	394	451	563	676	1804	11.275
134	111	167	223	279	335	391	447	558	670	1788	11.175
135	111	166	222	277	333	388	444	555	666	1776	11.1
136	110	165	220	275	330	385	441	551	661	1764	11.025
137	109	163	218	273	327	382	437	546	655	1748	10.925
138	108	162	217	271	325	379	434	542	651	1736	10.85
139	107	161	215	269	323	377	431	538	646	1724	10.775
140	107	160	214	267	321	374	428	535	642	1712	10.7
141	106	159	212	165	318	371	425	531	637	1700	10.525
142	105	158	211	263	316	369	422	527	633	1688	10.55
143	104	157	209	261	314	366	419	523	628	1676	10.475
144	104	156	208	260	312	364	416	520	624	1664	10.4
145	103	154	206	258	309	361	413	516	619	1652	10.325
146	102	153	205	256	307	358	410	512	615	1640	10.25
147	102	153	204	255	306	357	408	510	612	1632	10.2
148	101	151	202	253	303	354	405	506	607	1720	10.125
149	100	150	201	251	301	351	402	502	603	1608	10.05

Clock Settings

As so many people still use the old-style "sync" boxes (instead of an all-in-one computer), this chart will help you find the settings to run these classic drum machines and sequencers in sync with each other and other devices.

Instrument	SBX 80	SRC Clock	SRC Settings
Linn 9000	48	192	-
Linn LM2	48	192	ENA SW down
Oberheim	96	384	ENA SW down
Commodore	25	96	-
Simmonds	24	96	-
Fairlight	-	1536	TTL/OUT 2
EMU Drumulator	24	96	ENA SW down
Sequential Circuits	24	96	or midi
Roland TR-808/TR-909	24	96	ENA up, DIN SYNC
Korg	24	96	Din SYNC
Roland MSQ700	24	96	DIN SYNC or midi
Linn MKI	-	192	FSK
Roland MC202 Microcomposer	-	96	FSK
Yamaha QXI	-	96	FSK or MIDI

Pitch Frequency

Every note of music is a soundwave of a particular frequency which can be affected by EQ. Every note on the keyboard has a MIDI note number for the sequencer to use as the note's "name". These letters and numbers should soon become the producer's second language.

Pitch	Frequency	Key No.	Pitch	Frequency	Key No.	Pitch	Frequency	Key No.	Pitch	Frequency	Key No.
C1	65.81	36	E2	164.81	52	A♭3	415.30	68	C5	1016.50	84
C#2	69.30	37	F2	174.61	53	A3	440.00	69	C#5	1108.75	85
D1	73.94	38	F#2	185.00	54	B♭3	466.16	70	D5	1174.66	86
E♭1	77.78	39	G2	196.00	55	B3	493.88	71	E♭5	1244.51	87
E1	82.41	40	A♭2	207.65	56	C4	523.25	72	E5	1318.51	88
F1	87.31	41	A2	220.00	57	C#4	554.36	73	F5	1396.91	89
F#1	92.50	42	B♭2	233.08	58	D4	587.33	74	F#5	1479.98	90
G1	98.00	43	B2	246.94	59	E 4	622.25	75	G5	1567.98	91
A♭1	103.83	44	C3	261.63	60	E4	659.25	76	A♭5	1661.21	92
A1	110.00	45	C#3	277.18	61	F4	698.46	77	A5	1760.00	93
B♭1	116.54	46	D3	293.66	62	F#4	739.99	78	B♭5	1864.65	94
B1	123.47	47	E♭3	311.13	63	G4	783.79	79	B5	1975.33	95
C2	130.81	48	E3	329.63	64	A♭4	830.61	80	C6	2093.00	96
C#2	138.59	49	F3	349.23	65	A4	880.00	81			
D2	146.83	50	F#3	369.99	66	B♭4	832.33	82			
E♭2	155.56	51	G3	391.97	67	B4	987.77	83			

Pitch Ratios

"Time stretching" programs and "harmonizers" change the pitch without altering the tempo, or change the tempo without creating the "Mickey Mouse" effect.

Changes can be made by altering the ratios. For example, if you want to increase the pitch by one semitone without altering the tempo or length of the sample you need to use a ratio of 1.059:1. Similarly, if you want to decrease the pitch by one semitone without altering the tempo you must use a ratio of 0.94:1

Semitones	Up	Down
1	1.059	0.941
2	1.122	0.891
3	1.189	0.841
4	1.260	0.794
5	1.335	0.749
6	1.414	0.707
7	1.498	0.667
8	1.587	0.630
9	1.682	0.595
10	1.782	0.581
11	1.888	0.530

Pitch/Tape Speed Ratios

If you use a traditional reel-to-reel tape machine, these "varispeed" settings will allow you to work out new keys that result from key changes.

30 IPS			15 IPS		
Semitones	Up	Down	Semitones	Up	Down
1	31.77	28.32	1	15.89	14.16
2	33.68	26.72	2	16.83	13.37
3	35.67	25.23	3	17.84	12.62
4	37.80	23.82	4	18.90	11.91
5	40.05	22.47	5	20.03	11.24

Frequency/wavelength

Every note is a soundwave of some length which needs the physical space to be properly heard. This is why big rooms are more "boomy", and why small rooms sound so tight.

Frequency	Wavelength	Frequency	Wavelength
20Hz	17.03m	500	680mm
50	6.81	1KHz	340
100	3.41	10khz	34
125	2.72	20khz	1.7
250	1.36		

1. Do you have to move to London to get yourself a record deal?

It depends on when you're asking. There have been periods when the majors went looking for talent in other parts of the country (for example, Liverpool, Manchester, Bristol, Wales) but few A&R men will travel more than a few miles. The generally accepted answer is YES.

2. Do you get paid when your songs are played on the radio?

Yes. Payment rates are based on the number of people listening. A play on BBC Radio One can be worth nearly £100, while a play on a regional station might be worth only £5. Songwriters are paid through the PRS (Performing Rights Society), while the performers are paid through either PPL, PAMRA or other such organizations related to the Musicians Union.

3. How do I "clear" the samples I use?

You simply agree a fee/royalty and sign a contract with the sampled artist/songwriter. Unfortunately, finding the copyright holders and negotiating with them can be difficult business and may require the services of lawyers or specialists.

4. Should I put a copyright symbol (©) after my song titles on my CD?

It's no longer necessary. The symbol dates from before the "Berne Convention" on copyright. Nowadays, in the unlikely event of a dispute, the only important thing is prove WHEN the songs were written.

5. What's the best keyboard to buy?

One with both sampled and synthesized sounds, which has presets that you like and a large enough keyboard to play comfortably. Of course, no one keyboard has everything.

6. How much money does an artist make from each record sold?

Commonly, between 2p and 25p depending on the terms of the record deal. Album sales are often around 15-20p each, while singles will be closer to 2p each.

7. How much money do you make from a UK national Number One?

Once upon a time, a chart-topper made everybody rich. Now, it could mean anything. At Christmas it will probably involve over 250,000 sales and might give the artist £50,000 for one week's sales; a summer Number One, on the other hand, might be only 35,000 sales – not enough even enough to recoup a small advance.

8. How can I sell my music on the Internet?

It is perfectly possible to register your own domain name, set up your own site, and sell your own music on the site. However, without outside advertising it's hard to imagine many people finding you. You could also sign up to existing Intenet companies that will sell your music for you on their websites – peoplesound.com is one such example.

9. How do I get a job at a recording studio?
Just show up and ask. Most studios don't care about training, qualifications or experience. Most just want somebody who will make plenty of tea and coffee without complaining, work long hours for little or no money, and keep their mouths shut.

10. Do pop stars mime on TV, or are they really singing?
They're probably miming. It's rare to see a singer really singing on TV. Of course, there are some who will always do proper live performances, but these artists are few and far between.

11. Should I wait for the prices to drop before I buy my equipment?
Yes, but you might wait forever. If you want or need to get started now, then buy it now.

12. How do I get my song played on the radio?
Impress the radio station's playlist committee or a particular show's producer. This is very difficult to do, of course, and people called "pluggers" make a good living doing just that.

13. What is the "PRS"?
It stands for Performing Rights Society and is the national organization that collects songwriters' fees for music played in public. This includes radio, TV, shops and restaurants.

14. How can I get my songs "covered"?
With great difficulty. Britain is a nation of singer-songwriters and so most acts write their own material. If they do cover a new song, it will usually have been written by someone they already knew. Few unknowns get the chance to break into this arena.

15. Am I allowed to "cover" any song I want at any time?
If a song has already been commercially released and you cover it "faithfully" (without changing the words or the basic music) you will almost certainly be allowed to release it.

16. What happens if I have a hit without ever signing a publishing deal?
You make extra money. A publishing deal means the publisher is taking a percentage for himself. If you are lucky enough to reach the top without such a deal, you get to keep all the money yourself.

17. Is an "indie" label better than a "major"?
For some people, indies have more credibility, as they are seen to care more about the music and less about the money. Reality does not always agree.

18. Can the Dance Music/DJ phenomenon last forever?
Predictions about trends in music are made at the prophet's peril. But it does seem that, like rock 'n' roll, dance music and DJs will never die.

19. How can I soundproof my bedroom?
You probably can't. The famous Roland TR-909 bass drum, for example, can penetrate anything when played at a heavy volume. The best ideas may be to keep the volume down, pay off the neighbours, invite the neighbours round to dance, or move.

20. How do bands get chosen to support a bigger band on tour?
Usually by the record company and occasionally by the big-name artist. The decision will almost certainly be based on a marketing strategy (the main act's genre) and the support band will pay a

fee for the privilege. This is called a "buy-on".

21. How many songs will fit on a CD?
As many as you can fit into 74 minutes.

22. What is piracy?
The act of stealing an artist's work without any intention of paying for it.

23. How much does the record company make?
If it's a hit, a lot. A million-seller grosses more than $10 million and they get to keep most of that. If it's a miss, they might lose a lot of money.

24. How many records are sold in a year?
In 1999, total unit sales (based on returns from 76 different countries) amounted to 3.8 billion.

25. How much is the world's music business worth?
The global market was worth $38.5 billion in 1999.

26. Which computer grooves best?
The old Atari ST. It may be old and weak compared to a Mac or PC, but when it comes to tightness of grooves, it wins hands down.

27. Where can I get cracked software?
On the Internet.

28. What drum machine has the best bass drum?
The Roland TR-909. No question.

29. How do I get that "breathy" vocal sound?
Use a top-quality condenser microphone, compress it heavily and EQ it with extra hi-end.

30. Do recordable CD-Rs sound as good quality as normal CDs?
Probably not. Your digital audio card is unlikely to be as good as one used in a commercial CD plant. The CD burner itself is probably as good as the best.

31. Do radio microphones and wireless systems sound as good as those with leads?
If its a good-quality frequency-switching model and if your microphone or guitar is good in the first place.

32. What does A&R stand for?
Artists and Repertoire. "A&R men" choose the artists and their "repertoire" (the songs).

33. What does a music publisher actually do?
He pays money up front for a cut of royalties. He also tries to get your songs covered and tries to get your songs used in films/TV and in adverts.

34. Do record companies actually listen to the tapes I send them?
Yes, generally, but usually only the first 60 seconds.

35. Do I need a producer?
Yes, if you feel that you could use a different perspective. No, if you don't.

36. How much does a producer usually get?
Between 1 and 4 "points", and maybe an advance.

37. What are "points" in a record contract?
Percentage points. "3 points" is three percent of the total profit (usually after costs).

38. Do I really need a manager?
Yes, at some point you will need someone to speak for you. Perhaps you don't need one just now, if that point is still a long way off.

39. How much does a manager usually get?
20%.

40. What time IS love?
3 AM, apparently.

Access
Find an item of information.

ADC
Analogue-to-digital converter. A device which takes in analogue (electrical) information and converts it to digital (numeric) information.

Additive Synthesis
The process of building up a sound by adding harmonic wave shapes to a fundamental.

ADSR
Attack, decay, sustain, release. The most common envelope generator configuration on a synthesizer.

After Touch
See *Touch Sensitivity*.

Alphanumeric
Information consisting of letters and numbers.

Alphanumeric Keyboard
A keyboard with letters and numbers like a typewriter, or computer keyboard.

Algorithm
A logical progression of procedures that will lead to the end result. A diagram representing a computer program. In *FM* (frequency modulation) synthesis, a particular configuration of operators.

ALU
Arithmetic and logic unit. Part of a central processor that actually executes the operation requested by an input command.

Analogue ("analog")
Generally, sounds that are not digital. Something

not divided into numerical steps, but continuous. For example, the fraction one-third cannot be shown exactly on a digital calculator, though it can be accurately represented on a slide rule, which is analogue. An analogue waveform in an electric circuit corresponds exactly to the actual changes in air density produced by an amplifier/loudspeaker connected to it.

ASCII
American standard code for information exchange. This code has been developed to allow computers to communicate in a common language. Word processors use ASCII files for this.

Assembler Language
A language that is close to the original binary code of computers. The language includes symbolic machine language statements relating directly to the instruction and data formats of the computer. Used by advanced programmers.

Assignable
Capable of altered function. An "assignable" control may have several functions under to control of software.

Attack
The first phase of a control envelope. The time it takes for the envelope to rise from its initial low to its maximum level.

Audio Cassette Interface
A connection allowing ordinary cassette recorders to be connected to computers enabling memory to be dumped to audio cassette.

Advanced Integrated Synthesis (AI)
Korg's version of sample synthesis used on their M1

model and developed through the T and 01/W series. The sounds are produced by the Digital Waveform Generator System in which computer analysis determines the frequency components of the sampled sound and then reproduces them by creating a harmonic table. Aperiodic or irregular waveforms created by extraction of harmonically unrelated frequency components. Variable Digital Filters and Variable Digital Amplifiers then process these sounds.

Advanced Wave Modulation (AWM)
Yamaha's version of sample synthesis.

Aperiodic Waveform
A waveform which does not repeat its cycle at intervals.

Backup
A copy. Data should always be backed up to guard against loss or damage to the primary medium.

Bandwidth
The usable frequency response for a system.

BASIC
Beginner's All-purpose Symbolic Instruction Code – a high-level computer language developed in the 1950s at Dartmouth College, USA. Language used by many home computers.

Bit
In computing, a single binary character that can exist as a "0" or "1".

Boot
To "boot up" a system is to prepare it for action by loading the operating system.

Bubble Memory
A non-volatile memory device which stores numeric information safely even when the power is turned off. Information is stored as magnetic "bubbles" on a sliver of synthetic garnet.

Bug
An error in a computer program. Software is such a complex science that many programs are sold to the public before all of the errors (bugs) have been discovered. During use some of these bugs show up and the software has to be revised or "de-bugged".

Channel
The path whereby a signal is transmitted electronically from one point to another.

Carrier
A waveform that is modulated by another signal. In Yamaha's FM synthesizers it is the waveform from the carrier operators that is actually heard.

Chip
A micro-processor, usually a sliver of silicon on which circuits are etched.

Control Voltage (CV)
Electrical signal generated by a control device. Used to alter elements of a voltage-controlled device, such as a *VCO*, *VCF* or *VCA* on an analogue synthesizer.

CPU
Control processing unit. The primary unit of a computer that includes the circuits controlling the interpretation and execution of instructions.

Cross-Mod
Using one oscillator's audio frequency to modulate another. This produces complex harmonics and sidebands similar to ring modulators.

CRT
Cathode ray tube. A television-type screen.

Cursor
The blinking dot or line on a computer screen or synth LCD that indicates where the user is working on the screen.

Cut-off Frequency
The frequency around which a filter operates. On a VCF it can be varied by a control voltage.

Data
Information that defines a specific task. A computer program may be written to solve a particular type of problem but special data must be provided before an individual calculation can be computed.

DCB
Digital Communications Bus. This is a Multi-pin communications system used on some pre-MIDI products.

DCO
Digitally controlled oscillator. Virtually all modern synths use these highly stable systems.

Digital
Represented by numbers, usually binary, where any number can be represented by combinations of "0" and "1". Sonically, this refers to information stored in "bits" and not as a continuous wave.

Decay
The second stage in the ADSR envelope chain. The time the envelope waveform takes to fall from its maximum level to the sustain level.

Disk Drive
Digital memory storage device used to store and retrieve information. Consists of a magnetic head very close to a disk spinning a high speed.

Download/Dump
To transfer the memory contents of a computer by feeding the information in its memory to some external storage device.

Dynamic Range
The amplitude levels between which an instrument operates. A drum has a virtually infinite dynamic range, since its amplitude can be almost zero when hit gently and extremely loud when hit with severe force.

Edit
To alter a programmed group of settings of values.

Emphasis
See Feedback.

Envelope
The "shape" of a sound when displayed graphically. Typically of an ADSR pattern.

Envelope Generator
Device which produces a waveform of the above type to control the pitch of an amplifier.

Equalizer
Complex tone control that enables the user to control accurately a sound's timbral balance.

Feedback
The output of a particular circuit or device when sent back to the input. Feedback can be used to introduce resonance to a filter or flanger circuit.

Filter
Device that allows only certain frequencies of a signal to pass.

Flanging
Effect achieved by introducing a controlled amount of feedback from the output of a delay line to the input.

FM Synthesis
Sound synthesis technique that relies on the waveform produced when one or more sine wave (modulator) modulates another (carrier).

Fourier Analysis Synthesizer
Fourier's formula states that any complex waveform may be resolved into a fundamental plus a set number of harmonics. This formula is used to allow computers to compute the gaps between information supplied about harmonic envelopes. This technique can also be used to analyze and re-synthesize sampled waveforms.

Frequency Modulator
Control of a waveform's frequency by another signal.

Frequency
The number of events in a given time. For example, the number of vibrations per second.

Fundamental
The basic pitch of a note. The root harmonic on which other harmonics are built.

Gain
Factor by which a signal is amplified. Gain is normally measured in decibels (dB). An increase of 3 dB in gain doubles the volume.

Gate
Control signal indicating the time a note is held.

Glissando
Transition between one note and another in distinct steps, usually semitones of equal note length.

Graphics Display
A CRT or LCD screen for displaying graphics. These have to be high resolution to allow easy manipulation of complex waveforms and envelopes.

Graphic Equalizer
Tone control that enables individual frequency bands to be amplified (boost) or attenuated (cut).

Ground or Earth
Point of zero potential in an electrical circuit. Any device that is connected to earth is "grounded" and cannot become live.

Hard Copy
To print out on paper.

Hard Disk
See Disk Drive.

Hardware
A piece of "physical" equipment, such as circuitry or a keyboard. Sometimes called "firmware".

Harmonic
A sound with a frequency mathematically related to the fundamental. The simplest harmonic is one octave above the fundamental – if the fundamental frequency is F, then one octave above is two times F. Harmonics are also called "partials" or "overtones".

Harmonic Series
In a harmonic overtone series all the component tones are multiples of the fundamental root frequency. Thus, continuing the above example, the series goes F (fundamental), 2F (second harmonic), 3F (third harmonic), 4F (fourth harmonic), and so forth. A non-harmonic series can be anything that doesn't fit within that pattern.

Headroom
The gap between the peak working level on magnetic tape and the point at which the sound might actually distort In computer parlance, "having the headroom" means having sufficient spare computing power.

Hexadecimal
A code for counting on which 16 is used as the base. Used in low-level computer languages which are slow to write but very flexible and fast. MIDI system exclusive code is written in hexadecimal.

Hertz
The unit of frequency. One hertz represents one cycle per second. Abbreviated to Hz.

High Note Priority
In a voice-assignable instrument, if more notes are played and held than there are voices, the highest pitched notes will be the ones to sound.

High Pass Filter
Filter that attenuates all frequencies below the cut-off frequency.

Interface

Circuitry that has to be connected between certain devices before they can be connected together.

Initialize

The start-up procedure for computer systems that use peripheral units such as disk drives or printers. The initialization program sets up the starting conditions. Also used in modern synthesizers to reset the instrument to the state it was in when it left the factory, or to reset voices to average default parameters.

Joystick

Performance control that takes the form of a lever.

Keyboard Priority

System that determines what is heard when more notes are played that there are voices to play them.

Keyboard Tracking

The shifting of the filter's cut-off point in relation to where you play on the keyboard. If necessary, this capability can provide dramatically different tones at either end of the scale.

Last-Note Priority

In a voice-assignable instrument, this means that if more notes are played than there are voices, the last ones played are the last ones heard.

Layering

Combining sounds so that pressing a single note on the keyboard makes two or more distinct sounds play together.

LCD

Liquid Crystal Display. Display screen used on most modern synthesizers to show information.

LED

Light Emitting Diode. A small light on a control panel used to signify the status of a particular control.

LFO

Low frequency oscillator. This is used as a modulation source.

Low-note priority

In a voice-assignable instrument, this means that if more notes are played than there are voices, the lowest pitched notes will be the ones that sound.

Low-pass Filter

Filter that attenuates all frequencies above the cut-off frequency.

Load

To place a program into a computer's "live" *RAM* memory.

Machine Code

Binary language, the language of "0" and "1" used by all computers.

Mainframe

The main part of the computer – the CPU. In everyday use, "mainframe computer' refers to the large, ultra powerful computers operated by governments and multinational corporations in which the "main' element of the name distinguishes the unit from small satellite terminals which may be able to interface with it.

Memory

Circuitry used to store information.

Memory Protect

Switch or function that prevents accidental erasure of date stored in a memory.

Menu Driven

Software design in which the program offers a "menu" of choices whenever a decision is required.

MIDI

Musical Instrument Digital Interface. Originally developed in the early 1980s as a means of communication between computer-based synthesizers. Connections are made using a series of five-pin DIN sockets. MIDI has evolved to perform a multitude of tasks from simply controlling synthesizers and sequencing to the automation of mixing desks, tape machines, lighting systems and multi-media.

MIDI File
MIDI information stored in *ASCII* format which can be transferred between different computer programs and platforms. For example, a sequence composed on a Macintosh Cubase system can be saved as a MIDI file and subsequently loaded into any other MIDI sequencer on any other platform.

Microtone
A musical interval smaller than a semitone (the difference between two adjacent notes on the piano keyboard).

Microprocessor
The CPU of a computer. Built in layers on a microscopic chip of silicon. Many domestic appliances are now "microprocessor controlled", from video recorders to washing machines.

Modem
A modulation/demodulation device that allows computers to connect to telephone lines. This allows computers in remote locations to exchange information using the ASCII code.

Modifier
Device that acts on a signal and changes its character.

Modular
System built from separate, interchangeable units.

Modulation
The act of applying a control signal to an audio signal to change its character.

Module
Device that forms part of a modular system, such as a synthesizer without its own dedicated keyboard.

Monitor
A device used for observing or testing the operation of something e.g. a visual display screen connected to a computer or highly analytical loudspeakers enabling any sound in the audible spectrum to be heard with great fidelity and accuracy.

Monophonic
Capable of producing only one independent note or channel at a time.

Multiplexer
A device that takes input from several sources and delivers them in one high-speed stream of information.

Multi-sampling
The technique of sampling at different frequencies across the keyboard range.

Munchkinization
The effect of a single sample played over an entire keyboard when played outside of its own range. On the human voice, for example, as the pitch gets higher the sound becomes falsely altered. Such as sample played more than half an octave above the original pitch doesn't sound like someone singing at a higher pitch, but has the effect of a smaller or younger person singing.

Multiple Trigger
System that produces a pulse every time a new note is played.

Multi-timbral
A term popularized by the Sequential Circuits company that describes a synthesizer or module capable of splitting up its oscillators so that each can produce its own sounds simultaneously. Most modern synths are multi-timbral, although the complexity and "thickness' of the sound can be compromized.

Musique Concrete

The use of recorded extra-musical sounds (often with various distorting effects such as ring modulation) to create electronic music.

Negative Feedback

Sending an inverted portion of an output signal back to the input. Because it is inverted, the signal damps or cancels the resulting output. As opposed to *Positive Feedback* which does not invert the output portion and therefore reinforces the output. A practical illustration of positive feedback is the "howl round" caused by placing a microphone or guitar pickup in front of an amplifier loudspeaker to which it is connected.

Noise

A collection of random frequencies that produce unmusical sounds or any unwanted sound. The definition of noise can be very subjective as shown in this example. The late Keith Moon – drummer with legendary London rock band The Who – was listening to the rough mixes of his band's latest album at a rather high level on a "ghetto blaster' in the foyer of a five star American hotel. When asked by a member of the hotel's staff to "please turn that noise down", Moon requested that the manager accompany him to his penthouse suite whereupon he disappeared into a bedroom and closed the door. Seconds later there was an ear-shattering explosion and the bedroom door was blown off its hinges. A slightly dishevelled Moonie reappeared: "That, sir, is NOISE."

Noise Generator

Device used to synthesize sound with random frequency content. "White Noise" contains all frequencies; "Pink Noise" has the high frequencies filtered out. Useful for creating wind, breath and sea sounds, or for adding breath to wind and brass instrument sounds.

Nest

A program within a program.

Non-Volatile Memory

Circuitry that can store information even when the power is turned off. Usually requires a small battery.

Off-load

See Down Load.

One-shot

Single event, such as the triggering of an envelope generator.

On-line

Available for use. Being "on-line" means that a piece of information, a program or a computer peripheral is ready to be used. Also refers to a computer connected via a modem to the Internet.

Operating system ("OS")

A program (or series of programs) that allow a computer to operate before specific functions are loaded. On some older machines this is stored on a floppy disk and has to be loaded before the computer can be used. On modern equipment the OS is invariably stored in the computer's *ROM* (Read Only Memory) and is automatically loaded on when the machine is switched on.

Operator

A voice element in *FM synthesis*. Corresponds to a combination of voltage-controlled sine wave generator, envelope generator and voltage-controlled amplifier in *analogue synthesis*.

Oscillator

Circuit that generates a constantly repeating wave-form. The rate at which it repeats determines the pitch of the resulting sound.

Outboard

Term applied to signal processing by separate external effects units, such as reverbs, delays and compressors.

Overlay

A system of software design which allows long

programs to be written and stored on disk ready to be called when required. During operation, the part of the program currently in *RAM* (Random Access Memory) will automatically call the next part of the program currently in RAM, "overlaying' and erasing the earlier part of the program.

Overtones

Pure tones that form part of the make-up of a sound, but, unlike harmonics, are not simple multiples of the *fundamental.*

Parameter

A variable that can be defined or set to bring about a desired effect.

Parallel Modulators

Configuration where more than one modulator directly controls the same carrier.

Parametric Equaliser

Complex tone control that enables two or more frequency bands to be amplified or attenuated. Unlike a graphic equalizer, the frequencies and spans of these bands are variable by the user.

Patch

The way in which the elements of a synthesizer are connected together. In modern synthesizers, a patch can be stored in the instrument's memory for later recall by the user.

Patch Leads (Cords)

Connecting cables used to link the parts of a vintage modular synthesizer.

Partial

The individual sine wave components that make up a complex waveform's spectrum and therefore timbre.

PCM

Pulse Code Modulation. A recording and playback system for digital storage of sounds. Developed by Sony in the early 1980s for their PCM-F1 digital audio recorder on Betamax videotape.

Peaks

The highest and lowest points of a waveform.

Period

One complete cycle or vibration of a sound source.

Periodic Waveform

Wave that continuously repeats itself and therefore has definite pitch.

Phase

The relative displacement in time between the starting points of two or more waveforms of the same frequency.

Phase Distortion

Changes a wave's *partial* structure by altering the shape of the wave itself.

Phase Locked

Waveforms at the same point in a cycle. Two waveforms that reach the same point at the same time are said to be phase locked together.

Phase Filter Phase

A type of filter that shifts the phase of frequencies on one side of the cut off point.

Pink Noise

Noise signal that has been biased to that it contains equal amounts of signal over each octave of the audio spectrum.

Pitch

The parameters of sound related to a wave frequency.

Pitchbend

Raising or lowering the pitch of a note on a synthesizer, usually by a lever or wheel controller.

Pitch Envelope

Envelope that controls the pitch change of a source.

Pitch-To-Voltage Converter
Device that produces a voltage proportional to the frequency applied to it.

Polyphony
Playing more than one note at once. The number of voices a synth has. The original polyphonic synth were four, five, six or eight voice instruments. Now 16, 24, 32 voices are usual with 64 and 128 voice models available.

Port
Input/output socket used to connect one device to another, such as the modem and printer ports on a computer. Also a fortified wine that tends to give you a headache.

Portamento
Smooth change in frequency from one note to another as produced by sliding the finger up a violin string. Most synthesizers can also be programmed to achieved a similar effect.

Positive Feedback
See Negative Feedback.

Pre-set
A value (or set of values) that has been set at an instrument's design stage and therefore cannot be varied. Some models have pre-set patches which can be edited and stored in user memories.

Pressure Sensitivity
See Touch Sensitivity.

Programmable
Allowing the construction of user defined sounds.

Pulse Wave
Periodic waveform produced by an oscillator that exists in alternate high and low states. The width of this rectangular wave can usually be varied by a control signal to produce Pulse Width Modulation which produces a pleasing harmonic shifting effect.

Q
Another name for "resonance" in a filter. This is defined by the amount of boost or cut available at the filter's cut-off frequency. The width of this boost/cut curve is defined as the "Q" value – the higher the Q, the sharper the curve.

Quantize
To change a smooth shape into a series of discrete steps. When a sound is sampled, its waveform is effectively quantized to the sample-rate of the sampler. When data is recorded on a MIDI sequencer it is quantized. Quantization on digital sequencers is employed to shift notes (usually to correct timing errors) to the nearest selected note value.

QWERTY Keyboard
Typewriter-style keyboard used as a computer interface for all applications, so named from the sequence of the first six letters. Some European countries use the "AZERTY" alternative, where the first two letters are different.

RAM
Random Access Memory. The part of a computer's memory that can be accessed and written to by the user, and used to perform computations. RAM is the main measurement of computer power. Most synths have between 2 Mb and 32 Mb available; many modern computers can be equipped with in excess of 1 Gb of RAM.

RAM Pack/Card
memory expansion cartridge or card containing RAM which plugs directly into an instrument or computer.

Real Time
The storing of music on a sequencer as it is being played. The alternative is to use *Step Time*, in which notes are inserted one by one according to selected parameters.

Release
The final stage of an *ADSR* envelope. The time it

takes for the *envelope* to die away and return to its initial minimum position after the note has been released.

Reset Switch
A switch found on some microcomputers which completely wipes all RAM and resets the computer ready for "re-boot".

Resonance
See Q.

Ribbon Controller
Performance control device that makes the selected parameter – often pitch or modulation – rise and fall depending where on the ribbon your finger is positioned.

Roll-off
The rate at which a filter alternates frequencies on either side of its cut-off frequency.

ROM
Read Only Memory. A permanent memory system. Information stored in ROM cannot be accessed at random, but must be loaded into RAM before it can be used. ROM us used for the permanent and semi-permanent storage of information such as the operating system of a computer or synthesizer.

Ring Modulator
An electronic device which combines two input waveforms to produce one complex, harmonically rich output frequencies related to those input.

Sampling
The digital recording of sound into RAM, hard disk, digital audio tape or video tape.

Sample Rate
In musical applications, the rate at which a computer measures sound. The sound wave is measured a fixed number of times per second, the frequency of which is called the "sampling rate".

The higher the sampling rate, the more accurate the sample. For professional fidelity, the sampling rates chosen by the recording industry are between 40,000 and 50,000 times per second. The rate used for compact discs is 44,100 times per second (44.1 kHz) The audio bandwidth is approximately half the sample rate – for CDs that is in the region of 22 kHz.

SCSI
Small Computer Serial Interface. A multi-pin connector enabling a computer or instrument to access mass storage devices such as hard discs and CD-ROM drives. A vastly quicker system for communication than MIDI.

Sequencer
Device that can memorize and subsequently play back a predetermined string of pitch, controller and timing information. This information can be sent to any suitably equipped instrument (usually via MIDI) for automatic replay.

SMPTE
A time code protocol drawn up by the Society of Motion Picture and Television Engineers in 1967 for the synchronization of soundtracks to movies and video. Based on a 24-hour clock divided into hours, minutes, seconds and frames. There are four frame types devised to correspond to the running speeds of both US and European film and video formats. When synching to audio tape, any of these formats can be used, as long as they are not intermixed.

Software
A collective name for all computer programmes. Software instructs microprocessors to do specific tasks. Most synthesizers today are software-based, enabling new software "updates" to be written and loaded into the to increase its power and versatility and provide new features.

Step Time
The programming of sequencers by entering the

parameters of each separate note sequentially. A relatively method of making music which usually squashes any spontaneity.

Subtractive Synthesis
Method of synthesis which starts with a harmonically rich waveform and is then filtered to produce the required sound.

Sustain
The third phase of an ASDR envelope. The level the envelope maintains while the note is held.

Touch Sensitivity
The ability of an instrument to respond to the force with which the keyboard is played. This is sometimes confused with Velocity Sensitivity which is response to the speed at which the keys are pressed. This response can be used to control parameters such as modulation, filter cut-off in brightness and, on some instruments, to trigger different sounds, depending on how the keyboard is played.

Trigger
One-shot waveform that indicates when a note has been played. *See also Gate.*

Unison
Instruments or voices playing the same pitch. Unison mode on a polyphonic synth converts it into a powerful monophonic with all the oscillators synchronized.

VCA
Voltage Controlled Amplifier. An amplifier whose gain is directly proportional to the control voltage applied to it.

VCF
Voltage Controlled Filter. Filter with a cut-off frequency directly proportional to the control voltage applied to it.

VCO
Voltage Controlled Oscillator. Oscillator with a frequency directly proportional to the control voltage applied to it.

VDU
Visual Display Unit. Can take the form of a computer monitor or an *LCD* on a synthesizer.

Velocity
See Touch Sensitivity.

Voice Module
Complete set of circuits in a synthesizer used to produce a sound. A simple voice module can consist of *VCO, VCF, VCA* and an *Envelope Generator.*

Volatile Memory
Memory system (such as *RAM*) which requires power to retain the contents of its memory. When the power is switched off, its memory data is lost.

Wave
The shape of the graph which holds the information pertaining to a sound wave.

Waveform Memory
RAM or *ROM* holding information pertaining to a waveform.

Wavetable
A method of tabulating waveform data in computer memory that allows the user rapid access to any part of the information.

Write
To copy. To write to an internal memory location or a disk means to copy the information to that location for subsequent recall when required.

Index

A

A&R (artists and repertoire) 8-10, 11, 172, 174
Acid House 136
acoustic guitars 103
acoustic treatments, studio 72, 127, 173
A-DAT 112, 113
advances (money) 146
advertising industry 11, 143
Akai systems 16, 44, 140
AKG microphones 96, 105
Alchemy editing software (samplers/Mac) 42
Alesis systems 111, 112, 118, 130
Amp Farm simulator (Line 6) 75, 77
amplifiers 20
AMS Audioframe DAW 116
analogue synthesis 23
analogue-to-digital conversion (ADC) 20, 35, 36-7, 121, 122-3, 130
analogue v. digital 120-3
Antares systems 75, 77
Apple Macintosh 24, 42, 115, 116, 117, 118, 130, 132
    basics 165-9, 170
    Digidesign 60
ARP 2600 keyboard 138
Arrange Window (Cubase) 26-7
Arrange Window (Logic) 32-3
Artificial (Automatic) Double Tracking (ADT) 71
Atari ST computer 24, 128, 174
attack transients 41
audio cards, computer 118, 130-2
Audiosuite plug-ins 76
Audiowerk systems 130
automation of mix 58-62

B

backup of data 164
Baker, Arthur 91
bass guitars 15, 82, 104
Beatles 10, 11
Beck 45
Benitez, Jellybean 82, 91
Berio, Luciano 109
Betamax video 112
Beyer DT-100 headphones 100
binary numbers and sound resolution 36-7, 114, 132
"bit crushers" 76, 77
BitHeadz Unity virtual sampler 140
Bomb Factory plug-ins 77
Boss Dr Rhythm drums 139
brass, recording 102
breakout boxes 131, 133
Brown, James 47, 48
budgets 148
Bulletin Board Services (BBS) 152-3
business aspects 143-59, 172-4
buying, advice on 117, 118, 172, 173
    see also recording rooms/studios
Byrne, David 81

C

C1 plug-in (compressor) 69
Calrec microphones 96
cassette tape 19, 108
CD/CD-ROM 37, 143, 154
    dynamic range of 68
    "pick'n'mix" by post 156-7
    samples from 39, 41, 45
CD players, sampling rate of 34, 35
CDRs 174
channel faders (mixing) 55
channel split 87
charts 92, 143, 156
Chemical Brothers 46
Cher 75
chorusing 71
"clickola" 156
clipping 40
clocking 122-3
clubs, music outlets in 150, 151
Cobain, Kurt 68-9
collaborative music-making, virtual 153-4
compression 42, 65, 68-70
computers 12, 17, 21, 24, 114-22
    basics 36-7, 127, 130, 132, 163-9
    sampling 48
    virtual mixing/recording 60-2, 74-8, 79, 135
    see also digital technology; internet
condenser microphones 96-8
contracts 51, 144, 146-7, 174
control rooms 99
Cool Hero 90
copyright see legal considerations
"covering" songs 173
crossfading 44
Crow, Sheryl 98
Cubase VST see Steinberg systems
cut-and-boost EQ 67

D

daisychaining 24
DAT 39, 48, 82, 84, 112-13, 137
delay box/line 71
    echo trick 87
demo tapes 147-8
desks, mixing 52-62, 126, 134-6
Digidesign see ProTools systems
Digital Audio Workstations (DAWs) 116-17
digital signal processors (DSPs) 60, 74-5
digital technology 20, 23, 116, 120-3
    keyboards 138-40
    mixing 59, 60
    recording 101, 111, 131, 143
    sampling 16, 34-51, 95, 140-1
    see also computers; internet
digital-to-analogue conversion (DAC) 35, 36, 121, 131
direct injection boxes 14, 104
disco 90-1
dither 123, 132
DJs 9, 49, 50, 51, 90-1, 156
    sending music to 149-50

Dolby noise reduction 111
doubling (ADT) 71
DPTM Club (Fabric) 151
drivers, software 130
drums 82, 84, 87, 105-6, 174
    drum machines 47, 137-8
    samples 44, 47-8
dynamic microphones 96, 103
dynamic range of sampler 37
dynamics, compressor control of 68-9

E

editing on Cubase 30-1
editing software for sampling 42
EDP Wasp keyboards 138
effect return input 65
effects 21, 56, 60, 64-77, 86-7, 120, 137
Electro Voice microphones 96
E-Magic LOGIC systems 70, 77, 79, 117, 128, 130, 136, 170
    "Fat EQ" plug-in 66
    sequencers 32
    virtual mixers 17, 62
EMT Reverb Plate 72
EMU samplers 140
Eno, Brian 81, 89
equalization (EQ) 54-5, 65, 66-7, 86-7
expansion see noise gating
external key (noise gates) 70

F

faders 55, 84-5, 133
Fairlight systems 12, 42, 116
Fat Boy Slim 9
feedback 16, 71
FilterBank plug-in EQ 67
flanging 71
foldback 100-1
Freenet 155
freeware (WWW) 153
frequencies 67, 86-7
"Funky Drummer" loop (James Brown) 47, 48

G

gating 65, 70
gnutella.wego.com 155, 170
Gordy, Berry 146
Grandmaster Flash 142
group buttons (mixing) 55
guitars 14-15, 75, 82, 103-4

H

harmonic distortion 120
headphones 100-1
hi-fi systems, domestic, as monitors 127

I

indie record companies 173
input channels (mixing desks) 54-5, 64

instruments
    frequency ranges of 86, 87
    recording 102-6, 124
Internet 152-9, 172-3, 174
    as plug-in source 79, 137
    useful websites 169 (Mac) 170
    see also computers; digital technology

J

jack sockets 15
Jazzy B 47
jitter 122

K

keyboards 82
    choice of 138-40, 172
    and MIDI 23-4
Key Edit Window (Cubase) 30
keygroups, assigning samples to 43-4, 141
Koblo series plug-ins 77
Korg systems 132, 138, 140
Kraftwerk 23, 88, 89
Kurzweil K-2000 keyboard 140

L

Lanois, Daniel 89
latency 118
law see legal considerations
layering 88-9
leads 136
legal considerations 11, 143-4, 146-7
    copyright 39, 49-51, 144-5, 154-5, 157-9, 172
Lengehling Supertrack (Commodore) 24
levels in mix, control of 84-5, 107
Lexicon 960L reverb unit 75
libraries, sample 48
licensing agreements 148
limiters, dynamic 69
List Edit Window 31
live recording 94-113
live sampling 39
LOGIC see E-Magic LOGIC technology
looping 41, 46, 47-8
"loudness" controls 20, 82-3
loudspeakers see speakers
Love, Courtney 145

M

Mac computers see Apple Macintosh
McFerrin, Bobby 89
Mackie mixing desks 19, 54, 60
Madonna 93, 97
mains power conditioners 127
management deals 144, 174
Mark of the Unicorn see MOTU systems
Martin, George 89
mastering machines 111-12
master section (mixing desks) 56-7
"mic/line" switches 94

microphones 14, 16, 94-113, 124, 127, 174
Microsoft Windows OS 115, 116
MIDI 23-5, 116, 128-9, 132, 153
    sampling with 43-4
    software 26-32, 59, 60, 62, 77, 170
miming 173
MiniDisk recorders 39
MiniMoog/MemoryMoog keyboards 77, 138
mix busses 55
mixing 80-93, 162
    desks 12, 17, 19, 52-62, 126, 134-6
    effects 65-76
Moby 13
modulation 71
MondoMod 360-degree phase manipulation 78
monitoring systems 20, 56, 127
"mono-listen" level check 85
Moroder, Giorgio 90, 147
Motown studio 50
MOTU (Mark Of The Unicorn) systems 24, 42, 122, 128, 133
mp3.com 155, 156, 157-9, 170
multi-port MIDI interfaces 24
multi program modes 44
multisampling 41
multitimbral modules 24
multi-track tape 112
Musicians' Union 172
music industry see record companies
Mute label 13
mute/solo buttons (mixing) 55

N

Napster.com 154-5, 157-9
networking for self-promotion 150
Neumann microphones 94, 96
noise gating 65, 70
normalization 40
North Pole plug-in 77
Nuendo DAW (Steinberg) 117, 128

O

Oberheim Matrix keyboards 140
off-line plug-ins 77, 79
Orbit, William 93
orchestration 89
organs, electronic see synthesizers
OSCAR keyboards 138
Otari systems 20, 108
out-of-phase microphones 127
overdubbing 111

P

pad switches, microphone 102, 105
"P and D" see pressing and distribution
panning (mixing) 55, 85
parametric EQ 67
Pastorius, Jaco 104
"payola" 156
PCI see audio cards, computer
PCs see computers

Peel, John 149
PeopleSound.com 155
percussion 44, 82, 87, 106
performance program modes 44
Performing Rights Society 172, 173
Perry, Lee "Scratch" 90
phantom power (microphones) 98
phasing 71
pianos, electronic see synthesizers
piracy see legal considerations, copyright
plug-ins 21, 62, 66, 67, 69, 74-9, 137
PM Dawn 83
pop shields, microphone 98, 99, 101
PPG WAVE keyboard 77, 138
Premier plug-ins 76
pre-/post-fade modes (mixing) 55
Presley, Elvis 109-11
pressing and distribution deals ("P and D") 148
producers 12, 174
program modes (sampling) 44
Prophet 5 (Sequential Circuits) 77, 79, 138
ProTools systems (Digidesign) 17, 60, 62, 74, 115, 128, 132, 170
PZM microphones 96

Q

QUANT function (Cubase) 30-1
quantizing (digital audio) 122-3
Queen 58

R

radio outlets 149, 172, 173
ratio control 69, 70
real time plug-ins 77-9
Real World Studios 18
Rebirth 134
record companies
    contracts 51, 146-8, 150, 174
    and new markets 8-13, 90, 92, 143, 154-9
recording processes, new individual 12-13
recording rooms/studios 17-21, 53, 61
    setting up 99-100, 124-41
        see also buying, advice on
recording sessions, basics of 160-2
records as source material 39, 45-6
ReCycle software 46, 48
Red Valve virtual guitar amplifier 64
    see also Steinberg systems
remixing 90-3
resolution and digital sound 36-7
return channels 56, 65
reverb (reverberation) 72-3, 75, 85, 86-7
reverse sampling 42
rocketnetwork.com 153-4, 170
Rodgers, Nile 90
Roland
    drum machines 137, 138, 139, 174
    keyboards 138, 140
    samplers 140
rough cuts 41
royalties 146-7, 172
RTAS plug-ins 76

S

safety copies 146, 162
sample CD/CD-ROMs 39, 41, 48
sampling 16, 34-51, 79, 91, 129
    dedicated samplers 140
      see also Akai systems
Sanchez, Roger 51
saturation effect 120
saving work, importance of 40, 164
saxophones 102
scaling 40
Scour.com 155
selective synchronization ("sel-sync") 111
selling 12, 142-159, 172-3
Sennheiser microphones 96
sequencing 20-1, 22-5
    software 26-32, 128
shareware 153
    see also Internet
showcases 148-9, 157
Shure microphones 96, 105, 106
signal-to-noise ratio 40
sine waves 36-8
singers *see* vocalists
slapback 71
SMPTE inputs/outputs 24
SNAP function (Cubase) 31
Solid State Logic (SSL) 56, 59
songs *see* vocalists
Soul II Soul 47
Soundcraft 328 mixing desk 60
Sound Forge systems 128
soundproofing 127, 173
"sound warpers" 77
sourcing samples 39, 45-6
speakers 16, 20, 83, 127
Spears, Britney 154, 155
Spector, Phil 88-9
splitter boxes 101
Steinberg systems 64, 131
    Cubase VST 26-32, 75, 76-7, 117, 128, 136, 170
Strong Room Studios 53
Stubblefield, Clyde ("Funky Drummer") 105
studios *see* recording rooms/studios
synthesizers 15-16, 22-3, 39, 95, 118

T

"talent nights" 148-9
talent scouts 8-10, 11
talkback systems, studio 56
tape 19, 58, 108-113, 131, 157
threshold controls 69, 70
Time Bandit software 43
time-stretching samples 42
TOOLBOX (Cubase) 31
    see also Steinberg
Top 40 chart 92, 143
transients 48
TrueVerb (reverb) plug-in 73
trumpets/trombones 102
truncation 40-1

Tubby, King 90
tuning correction plug-ins 75, 76

U

Ultrapitch plug-in 78
UMI software (BBC) 24
Unity DS-1 software sampler 77
Universal v. mp3.com 159

V

Vasquez, Junior 91
Vega, Suzanne 89
Vegas DAW (Sonic Foundry) 116, 128
velocity crossfades 44
vinyl, cutting 57
virtual mixing 17, 60-2
virtual recording, collaborative 153-4
virtual record shops 155
Vision (Opcode) systems 128
visualization, mixers using 85
vocalists 71, 82, 84, 87, 89, 99-101, 109, 127, 162
    sampling song segments 39
voice assignment *see* keygroups
voltage-controlled oscillators (VCOs) 23
volume control 82-3
von Karajan, Herbert 108-9
VST *see* Steinberg systems

W

Waldorff Wave synthesizer 118
waveforms 36-8
Waves plug-ins 76
websites, useful *see* Internet
Wilson, Brian 11
Wintel boxes 116, 117, 132
work, finding studio 173

XYZ

Yamaha systems 24, 60, 127, 138, 140
ZOOM commands 41

ACKNOWLEDGEMENTS

The authors would like to thank the following people for their help with the project:

Jenny O, for making the connection; FX Rentals, for the use of the warehouse; Rob C, for the kickin' CD; Wayne Bardell for England; Terry B (Close to the Editor) and Adam "It's a Bad Crop" Wright; Nigel Frieda for years of good sessions; Grom, Stef and the "Grim Up North" Bradford Possee; J. S. Bach, Duke Ellington, Mozart, Beethoven, Stravinsky, Charlie Parker, Miles Davis, Jimi Hendrix, Peter Wolf, et al for connecting up the dots.

And most of all, Mish and Ange for Love, Peace, and Understanding.